Julian City
and
Cuyamaca Country

ALSO BY CHARLES LeMENAGER

OFF THE MAIN ROAD
A History of the Rancho Cañada
de San Vicente y Mesa del Padre Barona
ISBN 0-9611102-0-2 (1983)
Second Edition
ISBN 0-9611102-3-6 (1990)

RAMONA AND ROUND ABOUT
A History of San Diego County's
Little Known Back Country
ISBN 0-9611102-1-X Cloth
ISBN 0-9611102-2-8 PrBd (1989)

Julian City
and
Cuyamaca Country

A History and Guide to
The Past and Present

By

Charles R. LeMenager

Second Printing 1998
Third Printing 2001

Library of Congress Catalogue Card Number 92-81181

International Standard Book Number
Hardcover: 0-9611102-5-2
Perfect Bound: 0-9611102-4-4

Printed in the United States of America

Published by:

Eagle Peak Publishing Company
P.O. Box 1283
Ramona, California 92065

Cover design by Ernest Prinzhorn

iv

Table of Contents

MAPS   PAGE

Prologue

During the early 1870s when Col. L.B. Hopkins, miner, saddle maker and back country correspondent for the San Diego Daily World filed stories about happenings in the mining country, his dateline read *JULIAN CITY*.

In laying out the town and drawing in streets and lots in 1870, town father Drury Bailey called it *JULIAN CITY*. That's what people called the raw mining settlement in those early boom and bust times.

In later years the town was referred to in retrospect by other names. The illustrious editor of the Julian Sentinel from 1887 to 1893 and venerable town booster, James Jasper often wrote about it as *JULIAN CAMP*. While Horace Wilcox, who settled in Julian at the height of the boom at age 28, and lived to talk about it well into the 1930s, called it *"a rag-house minin' town"*.

At no time during the nineteenth century, could Julian, Banner and Cuyamaca City combined, ever boast a population exceeding 600. But *JULIAN CITY* is what it was called in the early days, so that's how we'll refer to it in

7

its historical context.

It has always been an integral part of the Cuyamaca mountain country. To try to write a story just about Julian's past without bringing in the lore of its surrounding mountains is impossible. The heritage is too intermingled. There'd be too many holes in the historical fabric.

In pulling together information for a broadly based history such as I have attempted here, the researcher is ever on the look-out for every bit of information he can get his hands on. Like Julian miners in the 1870s, I have prospected wherever there was a lead. Sometimes the "diggins" are encouraging and helpful, occasionally they are very rich. Some of the best paydirt found has been contained in unpublished writings.

Gale W. Sheldon did an excellent job of tracing Julian's early history while working on his master's thesis at San Diego State College (now University) in 1957-58. His work titled *JULIAN GOLD MINING DAYS* runs 284 typewritten pages. This unpublished paper can be reviewed at the University's library.

Another rich source of local lore is found in two manuscripts by James Jasper. While his writings are more colorful, and in a few cases run more toward story-telling than scholarly reporting, they none the less contain a great deal of useful facts. He intended to have these works published, but for reasons we tell about later, they never were. *JULIAN AND ROUND-ABOUT* was written in 1928, and *TRAIL-BREAKERS AND HISTORY MAKERS* in 1934. The latter can be found at the San Diego Historical Society's library in Balboa Park, San Diego.

Civil War history fascinates me, as it does many others. It was a lot of fun to be able to trace the Julian and Bailey brothers' war records at the Georgia Department of History and Archives and in North Carolina documents. Putting those records into context has been most educational for me, and I hope you find them interesting too.

Other notable sources, which have been published, include the works of Judge Benjamin Hayes, Hero Rensch and Arthur Woodward about Indians and the Mexican period and Helen Ellsberg about Julian mining history.

JULIAN CITY AND CUYAMACA COUNTRY is my third effort at recording a few pieces of history about San Diego County's heartland. The first book, *OFF THE MAIN ROAD* covered the San Vicente and Barona Valley's past. Its general geographic boundaries were the old Mexican land grant which today encompasses the planned community of San Diego Country Estates and the Barona Indian reservation.

The second, *RAMONA AND ROUND ABOUT* traced the history of the old Santa Maria and Santa Ysabel Ranchos, and territory in between.

With completion of this book, I have finished what I like to call my San Diego back country historical trilogy.

There are several parts in this book, however, that I don't feel comfortable about. Picture captions that don't have complete lists of names, and stories that have only vague details. Unfortunately one can't wait to publish a history book until he has every detail. If he did there would be nothing published. Too much material is either unavailable, undiscovered or has been lost over the years.

We expect to have another printing of this book. I invite the reader to call me on any errors and fill me in on some of the blank spots we missed that he may be

able to furnish.   In the meantime, we hope you enjoy
the book and derive a fraction of the pleasure reading it
as we did in putting it together.

San Vicente Valley   CRL
Ramona, California
May, 1992

1

Setting

Much of Julian's appeal today lies in the image of a frontier town. Pioneer storefronts provide an almost movie set quality to its Main Street,

The town site is nestled at 4,500 foot elevation, in a saddle between the northern end of the Cuyamaca range and the south slope of Volcan Mountain. It is located about 50 miles northeast of downtown San Diego and reached by freeway and fairly good country roads.

Julian started as a mining camp, much like many others spawned by the gold fever pervading California during the mid to late 1800s. Unlike most such camps, however, it didn't disappear after the mines played out. The Julian area had more going for it than mere gold. It has good climate and good soil and is close enough to one of California's fairer cities to provide those so inclined, with opportunities for a broader life style.

Julian continued to play a significant role in San Diego County primarily because of its agriculture and livability. But while it was estimated there were 300 miners

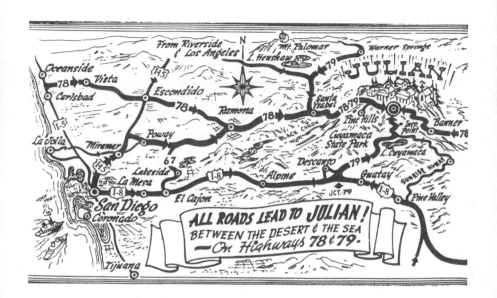

MAP USED BY THE JULIAN CHAMBER OF COMMERCE for many
years during the 1950s and 60s. It's as good today as it was 40 years ago.
Geographically the town hasn't changed a bit. The main highways have
however, and we have taken the liberty here of altering their designations
accordingly. Old highway 80 is now Interstate 8, 101 is I-5 and 395 is I-15.

working the area in the summer of 1872, the town
counted only 50 houses, 3 hotels, 4 stores, 2 restaurants,
1 schoolhouse and the "usual number of saloons". Far cry
from any city.

At the height of gold mining activity, people were
spread throughout the hills from Banner in the east and
Stonewall to the south. At no time during that era did
population exceed 600. Today's population of about
1,200 (1990 census) reflects residential building in the

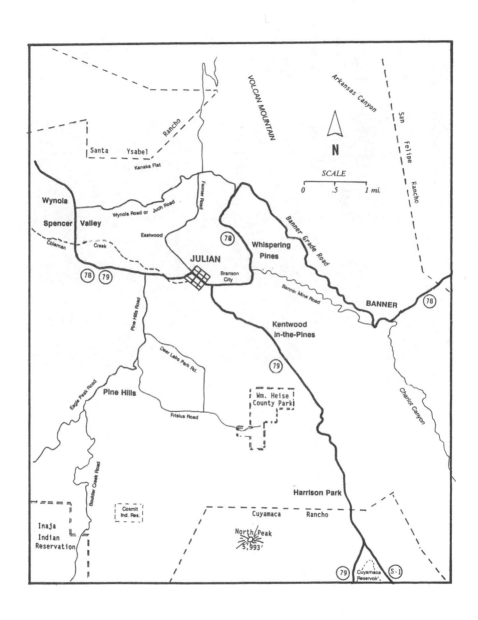

JULIAN AND VICINITY

AERIAL VIEW OF JULIAN 1992, looking north.

outlying areas like Pine Hills, Whispering Pines, Kentwood in the Pines, Wynola and Harrison Park

But the permanent residents are vastly out numbered on week ends, especially during the fall. That's when hundreds, to even thousands of flat-landers converge on the town to just stroll around, sample some apple pie and attend any number of special events.

Julian, like many gold mining towns, has been romanticized over the years with tall tales. Upon investigation into official records, however, some of these stories turn out to have no basis of truth. One is that in its hay-day, Julian out populated the city of San Diego. A simple check of census figures discredits that one.

CUYAMACA'S THREE PROMINENT PEAKS dominate the eastern skyline as viewed from San Vicente Valley west of the San Diego River basin. North Peak on the left is 5,993' high, Middle Peak is 5,883' while Cuyamaca Peak, or South Peak on the right is the tallest at 6,512'. In the foreground, Eagle Peak stands 3,226' high.

Another one has Julian and San Diego vying for the site of San Diego County's seat of government in the early 1870s. That's just another fable, and we'll tell you how it got started later in this book.

Cuyamaca Country stretches from Julian all the way south to the pretty little community of Descanso, just north of busy Interstate 8.

Cuyamaca Rancho State Park covers most of the territory in between. It has been part of the California Park system since the early 1930s. Its campgrounds and hiking trails provide a welcome retreat for residents of California's second largest city, San Diego. As well it does for people from all over.

Just north of the State Park is Lake Cuyamaca, a popular place for fishing and duck hunters since shortly after it was created in 1887. Nearby is the Stonewall Mine exhibit and site of old Cuyamaca City, which has been torn down and gone for over sixty years. The Boy Scouts have their Camp Hual-Cu-Cuish near the lake and throughout the Cuyamaca and Volcan mountain area there are found many other youth and summer camps.

The setting for this book is a unique one. Downhill on one side is an exploding seaside metropolitan area. Downhill to the east is the beautiful, peaceful desert region of Borrego and Imperial Valley.

JULIAN CITY AND CUYAMACA COUNTRY has four seasons. Winter brings snow, frozen pipes and lots of visitors. Spring brings green grass, blooming tulips, daffodils, lilacs, apple blossoms and lots of visitors. Summer brings hot days, cool nights and lots of visitors. And fall, that's even a bit more unique. It brings ripening apples and pears, crisp and spicy air and a WHOLE LOT of visitors.

But what would Julian be without those visitors. Some residents complain about the congestion on the weekends. Obviously they're the spoilsports who've already made their stack. Most Julianites, however, welcome the visitors and work hard to bring 'em back. After all, they pretty much have the country to themselves on the other five days of the week.

2
Indians

The Cuyamaca State Park campgrounds in Green Valley and Paso Picacho have been home to campers since prehistoric times. The setting has changed little. Today's campers even bear a few similarities to their aboriginal predecessors. They cook over open fires, sing songs and tell tales and some of them even sleep in big rubber tired "wigwams" bearing such Indian names as Winnabago, Brave and Chief. But similarities in the life style of the early natives and today's outdoorsmen, with their motorhomes and camping conveniences, are worlds apart.

A common attraction remains, however. That is the natural resources that drew early people to the Cuyamacas. The abundance of water, trees and plants, are the same features that attract man to these mountains today.

Few other areas in all California had as many Indian village sites in such close proximity as have been found in the Cuyamaca area. Just within the old Mexican land

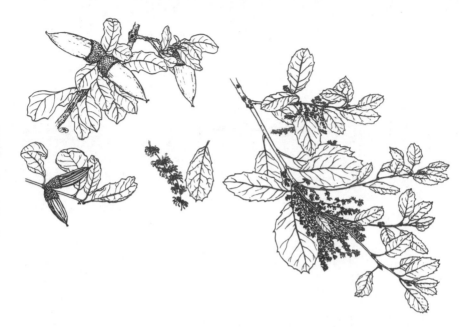

ACORNS were the main food staple in the Kumeyaay Indian's diet. The *Quercus agrifolia,* or Coast Live Oak grew in abundance in the Cuyamacas.

grant boundaries alone, which extends a bit beyond park limits, more than fifteen distinct pre-historic villages have been identified.

Before the Spanish arrived in the sixteenth century, it is believed over 1,000 natives lived there during the temperate, gathering seasons which lasted from late spring through autumn. When white men came in the 16th century, and began introducing their unique diseases into this new-world environment; and when they later moved their grazing and farming onto the Indian's hunting and gathering lands, the native population began its steady decline to near extinction.

Archaeologists have found evidence of Indian occupation 3,000 to 7,000 years ago in the deserts east of the Cuyamacas. It can only be assumed that early man

THE BLACK OAK, or *Quercus kelloggii* acorns were the Indians' favorite type. Like other acorns, they were gathered in the fall.

flourished that long ago in the Cuyamacas as well.

Relatively few professional archeological digs have been done to verify periods of occupation there, however. This is unfortunate since these mountains are considered to have been one of the most abundant areas for hunters and gatherers in southern California.

"The Cuyamaca environment provided the best of all worlds for the Indians. There was permanence in the food supply without need for farming," said Dr. Delbert True, who is one of the few archaeologists to have done any extensive exploration there. *"There was a wide enough range of plants and animals so that if one food source failed, there were backups. The peoples who inhabited these mountains came as close to being secure as any hunter/gatherer group in the world."*

Some anthropologists, however, believe these people practiced extensive plant husbandry, citing evidence of cultivation of oak, pine, manzanita and different types of shrubs and bushes, and also conducting controlled burns to manage their habitat.

While it may be shown that a few individuals experimented in planting something, this happened mainly after the arrival of the white man. According to Dr. True, these Indians, as a people were not an agrarian society. Farming was not necessary, since natural food supplies were in abundance in this environment.

Many species of oak trees abound with acorns, as well as pines furnishing nuts, wild grasses bearing seeds, elderberry and coffee berry shrubs and manzanita. Grass seeds were harvested in late spring, shrubs bore berries during the summer and in the fall acorns and pine nuts kept the natives well stocked.

Vast numbers of deer, rabbit and wood rat furnished meat for the hunters. Old timers interviewed during the 1920s, recalled earlier days when they saw trout swimming in the upper reaches of a Sweetwater River that flowed rapidly year round during wet years.

The name, Cuyamaca comes from the Indian language and has been known to white men for at least 165 years. The first written mention being found in a San Diego Mission report by Father Jose Sanchez dated 1827.

The Indian form of Cuyamaca was Ah-ha Kwe-ah-mac (Water Beyond) or "Rain Behind". The Spanish version of the name dropped the first two syllables and added the euphonious "a" at the end, CUYAMACA. The Spanish and Mexicans used the name to designate both the mountains and region in general.

While the name Cuyamaca did not appear in writing before 1827, white men were familiar with the area as early as 1782. In April that year, Pedro Fages,

California's Spanish military commander and governor, lead a company of twenty Spanish soldiers back to San Diego from a second unsuccessful attempt to subdue the Yuma Indians on the Colorado River. At the junction of San Felipe and Carrizo creeks, where Juan Bautista de Anza had camped in 1774 and 1775, Fages took a new route. Instead of following Anza's trail by way of Borrego Valley, they proceeded through Mason Valley, and from there followed an old Indian trail up the Oriflamme Canyon. Narrow trails led them "from hilltop to hilltop", through what later became known as Cuyamaca and Green Valleys, by the Cuyamaca and Mitaragui Indian villages, to the village of Jamatayune located just north of today's Guatay. Another mere thread of a trail took them down the hills to the Viejas grade.

Fages stated his motive for the divergence in a diary entry dated April 17th: *"Hearing that the Indians in the mountains about San Diego were in a state of semi-insurrection, I thought I might observe their movements and make them feel some respect if I should change my route and pass through their territory on my way."*

Fages found the mountain Indians to be friendly. *"They approached me very pleasantly"*, he wrote. Giving them glass beads, he recorded that they bore no arms and seemed very contented. He called them "Camillares".

The description Fages gave of the area is significant:

"There were numerous groves of pine and other trees in the entire neighborhood, also a great deal of pasture in the canyons between the hills ... and plenty of water."

For hundreds of years before the appearance of Fages, Indians built their mountain camps beside streams and sheltered springs where acorns and pine nuts were plentiful. The micro-climate zones they selected were usually mild, except during winter months. Then it was just a short trip down the slopes to the warmer climes. The Descanso area to the south was favored, as well as the desert to the east. In the desert they bathed in the same hot spring waters known by today's campers as Aqua Caliente County Park.

They would periodically travel the westward trails to the sea to enrich their diets with sea food. They knew when the smelt spawned and where on the beaches to gather those fish each year. They also traded their deer skins and seeds for prized abalone and olivella shells.

This network of ancient Indian trails, leading from desert to mountain and from mountain to seashore, provided the first white man with a road map for his ultimate conquest of the Indian's homelands.

Archeological digs of former Cuyamaca village sites reveal much about the travel and trading activities of these early people. Artifacts coming from these sites include imported materials such as clays for making pottery brought from the desert, obsidian from the Salton Sea area, and beads and ornaments made from shell from the Gulf of California.

Anthropologists and ethnologists classify Indian tribes by the languages and dialects spoken. The Indian peoples who inhabited the Cuyamacas are generally referred to as KWAAYMII. Their's was a subdivision within a broader grouping known as KUMEYAAY who occupied a vast area stretching from the Pacific Ocean to the desert of today's Imperial County. The northern boundary line of this area ran roughly from Oceanside through Julian and the lower part of the Salton Sea.

Until recently, Indians who occupied the Cuyamacas and territory south and west of there, were referred to by ethnologists as Southern Dieguenos. However, during recent times, there has been controversy over their proper designation. While there's still not total agreement, KUMEYAAY receives the greatest acceptance today.

PLACE NAMES

Those concerned today with conserving our cultural resources don't like to publically identify specific locations of early Indian villages and camps. For good reason. Many of these sites have been violated by "pot-hunters", people who illegally dig for artifacts. In their zeal to unearth and pilfer pots and arrow heads they have done little to add to scientific knowledge. On the contrary, they only disturb the sites, making it harder for anthropologists to study and record an accurate picture of how these prehistoric people lived there.

So don't be surprised there are no painted signs in the park marking exact locations of the Indian places we talk about here. If you are a careful observer, however, you'll be able to know when you're on or near a site of former Indian occupation. The most obvious sign is a large rock outcropping that has several holes, or indentations six to ten inches in diameter. It will be close to oak trees, and often near a water source. These holes are called bed rock mortars and are where Indian women ground their acorns. If you are especially perceptive, you may discover a "slick" on one of these outcroppings. This would be an area that is smooth to the touch, indicating small wild grains and seeds were ground there. As you sit on this rock, you may get some idea of what the Indian's food preparation facility was like. You may even imagine the bird-like chatter of native women busy grinding, and the laughter of dark-skinned children playing on near-by rocks.

The dozen, or so known Indian rancherias that were located within the boundaries of Rancho Cuyamaca had

A BED-ROCK ACORN GRINDING station, typical of many found near former Indian village sites in the Cuyamaca Mountains. Here early day squaws sat and prepared their most important food staple. The deeper holes were used to soak the acorns to remove the bitter tannic acid. Shallower holes were for grinding the acorns into meal. This rather large one, with thirteen holes, is being inspected by Sylvan Ferland, a contemporary native.

common characteristics.

In addition to being close to a reliable source of water, there is often a meadow or open area in the forest where they set up their jacales, or huts, thatched with

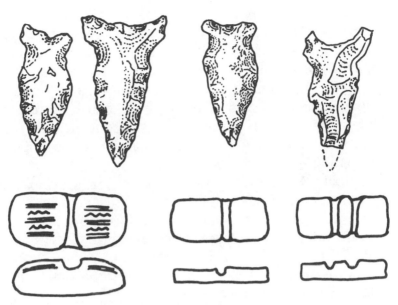

ARTIFACTS uncovered during an archaeological excavation at one of the Huacupin village sites in 1962 included arrow points and shaft straighteners. The points were fashioned from basalt or felsitic stone. The strightenerers were used for compound arrow shafts made from cane and hardwood, since longer pieces of hardwood weren't available. These were joined with tar or pine pitch. The steatite (soapstone) devices were heated and the arrow shafts pulled through the joined stones to remove kinks in the shaft joints.

he-wat, deer weed. These sites were comparitively warmer, sheltered places protected from prevailing winds and with sunny exposure, even when located on a northern slope, such as the Ah-ha kwe-a-mac (Cuyamaca) village site.

RANCHERIA SITES

Twelve distinct Indian village sites, or as the Spanish called them, rancherias, have been identified within the boundaries of Cuyamaca Rancho State Park. Most of these villages had been abandoned by 1870 when they were identified and located for public record by Judge Benjamin Hayes. Hayes was working as attorney for the Julian settlers in the Rancho Cuyamaca boundary fight. (More about that later.) His work in this regard not only helped define the correct boundaries of the contested grant lands, but in so doing, has also provided the historian invaluable information about early man's occupation of the area.

Beginning in the north the villages were: Cuyamaca, Jual-cu-cuilsch, Pisclimi or Pisclim, Pilcha, Mitaragui, Pam-mum Ah-wah, and the five mesitas of Huacupin.

Four additional villages have been identified just outside park boundaries, but within or near the confines of the old Rancho Cuyamaca. They were, Yguai, Inaja, Jamatayune, and Guatay.

CUYAMACA: The ancient village of Cuyamaca, or AH-HA KWE-A-MAC, was the most populous of all the rancherias in this region. Located at the foot of the long north slope of Stonewall Peak, it was one of the main villages on the primary north-south Indian trail that ran north through Jamatajune, over the east mesa, through Green and Cuyamaca valleys and over the east brow of North Peak past the village of Yguai on the way to Santa Ysabel. Observant hikers and riders will encounter subtle remnants of this village in and around the Los Caballos horse camp.

Long after the Franciscans established their mission system, this village was home to San Diego area's largest unconverted Indian populations. These natives were an independent people whom the mission padres were never able to control. They kept aloof from both the white settlers and the Christianized Indians of San Felipe and Santa Ysabel.

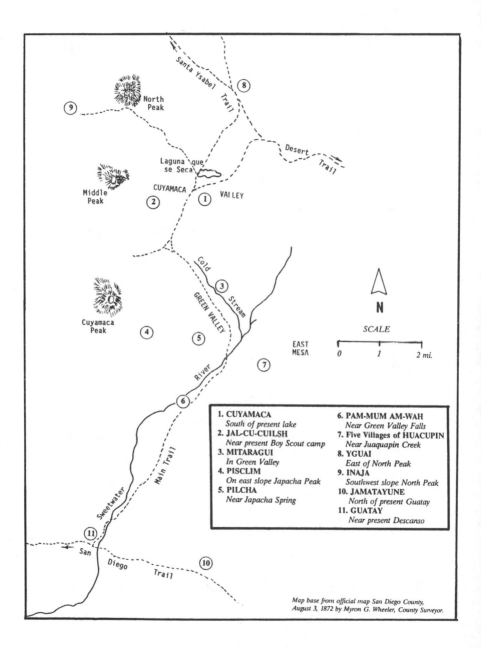

1. CUYAMACA
   South of present lake
2. JAL-CU-CUILSH
   Near present Boy Scout camp
3. MITARAGUI
   In Green Valley
4. PISCLIM
   On east slope Japacha Peak
5. PILCHA
   Near Japacha Spring
6. PAM-MUM AM-WAH
   Near Green Valley Falls
7. Five Villages of HUACUPIN
   Near Juaquapin Creek
8. YGUAI
   East of North Peak
9. INAJA
   Southwest slope North Peak
10. JAMATAYUNE
    North of present Guatay
11. GUATAY
    Near present Descanso

Map base from official map San Diego County,
August 3, 1872 by Myron G. Wheeler, County Surveyor.

ANCIENT INDIAN VILLAGE SITES
IN THE CUYAMACA MOUNTAINS

The years 1825 to 1837 were marked by Indian restlessness and attacks upon white settlements. These mountain Indians showed hostile resentment for the encroaching Spanish occupying some of their best lands. In 1837, four white men were killed and three white girls kidnapped at Pio Pico's Rancho Jamul. A military expedition of eighteen soldiers and thirty friendly Indians was dispatched to subdue the rebels. They proceeded to the Cuyamaca Mountains but met no resistance at Jamatajune or at Guatay. At the village of Cuyamaca, however, Vicente Romero, a member of the detachment related:

"The Indians were more numerous than at any other place... we had to fight... killed some of them. They finally submitted to our terms, promising not to molest the settlements further. We remained here in all about five days."

JAL-CU-CUILSH: This village, together with Cuyamaca and Yguai, faced the broad meadows of Cuyamaca valley and formed a large cultural center.

Under spreading live oak trees near the Boy Scout's Hual-Cu-Cuish Camp lodge, community metates of this ancient village may still be seen. For many years, Scouts have been holding their council fires next to one of the village's larger grinding stations. Trails leading up Middle Peak from this area lead to sites of smaller Indian camps which once were part of the village complex. The Azalea Trail, which is also accessed from Paso Picacho Campground is such a former Indian trail and is in flower in late May.

This village complex took its name from the Middle Peak of the Cuyamaca group which the Indians called JUAL-CU-CUILSH (or HAL-KWO-KWILSH), meaning "tough strong'. It was one of the names in a story, the

FROM PRE-HISTORIC times, the small green oasis at Vallecito was a favorite Indian winter camp. During the 1840s and 50s it was a welcome stop for pioneers on the way to California. It served as a Butterfield Overland Stage station from 1858 to 61. But the Indians never entirely abondoned it and as late as 1873 there were over 100 living there. This sketch, made there by John Woodhouse Audubon in 1849, shows the typical Kumeyaay jacale (hut).

legendary account of the "Battle of the Peaks" told by Maria Alto. While a fierce pre-historic battle raged among the mountains in the fable, old Jual-cu-cuilsh proved to be so formidable that he earned his title of "tough strong". The Indians who included this among their tribal tales about the old mountain, named their village after him.

These villagers, along with those from the Cuyamaca and Yguai rancherias provided a center where Indians from far and near came to periodically trade and hold great games. They came from the seacoast, from the desert and mountains for this annual event. A form of football was played and other contests of skill and prowess pitted one against another. These gatherings were to the early Indians what the Olympics mean today.

MITARAGUI: Located about three quarters of a mile south of the entrance to Paso Picacho campground on the Cold Stream trail is the site of Mitaragui village. Here the Indians had chosen a favored spot for their summer camp. It lay at the head of a long green valley where it was snugly sheltered from prevailing winds by the South Peak on the west, by Stonewall Peak on the north and on the east by the hills that enclose Harper's Valley. Mitaragui, meant "Crooked Land" in the Indian's language. It was on the main trail linking the villages on the East Mesa with those to the north.

The village of Mitaragui was abandoned by the natives sometime before 1856. John Westley Mulkins, step-son of James R. Lassator, told Judge Hayes in 1870 of how Mitaragui became Green Valley Ranch. The hereditary chieftain of the tribe claimed proprietary right to the village site and 160 acres of land lying to the south. Mulkins claimed to have negotiated purchase of the land from the chieftain for Lassator in 1857.

While there was no Indian occupation of the village in 1856, it apparently was quite active ten years earlier. In 1847, Cesario Walker entered into an agreement with Augustin Olvera to establish a water saw-mill and cut timber in close proximity to the village. Walker soon abandoned the place due to fear of the Indians who "made kind of revolution"

The Lassator/Mulkins Green Valley ranch house site is situated a few hundred yards south of the State park headquarters, where Cold Stream Creek and Sweetwater River meet. Little remains today to distinguish the site.

When Judge Hayes stopped at the ranch house in July 1870, the old chieftain, who was said to have sold the land to Lassator, was working in Mulkins' garden.

PISCLIM: Just below Japacha Peak, lies a small meadow covered with wild buckwheat. At the upper end of the meadow, where the soil is black, there is an immense boulder, flat and sloping to the south. In it are 45 deeply worn grinding holes. Next to it is another with five more holes. A third boulder, a small "family" community shaded by oak trees, lies at the northeast edge of the meadow. Here is where Pisclim, another important village, was located.

PILCHA: Located on the west mesa, overlooking Green Valley and the State Park head- quarters is Pilcha, also known as the Arrow Makers' camp. This site shows evidence of very early Indian occupation, and in modern times has seen considerable legal and illegal excavation, mostly the former. As recently as 40 years ago, white quartz crystals and obsidian flakes littered the surface of the ground, confirming activity of ancient arrow makers' activities. Many ollas (pots), burial urns, beads, arrow straighteners and other artifacts have been taken from this camp. Today these items form much of the collection at the park museum.

PAM-MUM AM-WAH: The site of this village was located within the present Green Valley Camp/Picnic Area of the State park. The Indians obviously chose this area for its sheltered meadow and abundance of live oaks. Here is where the Sweetwater River turns sharply to the west, dropping down over huge boulders forming the Green Valley Falls. In earlier days, beavers built their dams at this point in the river.

Probably only the second white man to settle in Green Valley was John Carl Eschrich, a native of Germany, who camped there from February to August 1856. A

veteran of Stevenson's New York Volunteers who came
to California in 1847, he had been a musician with the
regiment. Eschrich testified in the Cuyamaca boundary
case in 1873, that he camped there, at the site of
"Pamauaua", not far from the rancheria of Mitaragui.
His statement indicated that the Indians no longer were
occupying this site at the time of his arrival.

MESA de HUACUPIN: A hike up the Juaquapin Trail
to East Mesa or Mesa de Huacupin will take one past
five small village sites. The first, or lowest site was called
Hua-cu-pin, and gave its name to the Mesa de Huacupin
in days before the white man renamed it East Mesa.
   It apparently was still occupied when Hayes visited in
1870, for he wrote:
   *"The little rancherias, five in number, are in a long
wooded canon leading from Green Valley to the mesa of
this name. The first we approach is well sheltered by the
hills from the winter blasts and gives its name to the whole
mesa. They rise, one above the other, each with its own
little flat (masita) with water and a tolerably good patch
for cultivation, and each with its peach trees ... What stock
the Indians may have, ranges with that of shepherds and
coast stock raisers on the top of the mesa."*
   In 1950, Cuyamaca Rancho State Park Curator Hero
Eugene Rensch described the setting:
   *"... the first "mesita" is a good sized meadow above
which the village site of Huacupin was located. Out of the
meadow, a happy little stream (Juaquapin Creek) jumps
down through deeply cut walls overgrown by trees and
shrubs. Lush water cress grows near a tiny waterfall. High
on the banks on either side of the stream are the big
boulders with their deeply worn grinding holes. Some family
sites are almost hidden under the overhanging branches of
live oak trees which grow on the north side of the canada*

where the trail comes up over the brow of the hill."

"Down in the moist meadow, the Indians had their gardens of melons, beans, corn and squash. Somewhere there was a peach tree, the parent seed of which was brought from the mission gardens at San Diego. There were more gardens and other fruit trees on the higher mesitas. Only one of the trees is left today (1950)."

Huacupin meant "warm house" in their language, but that apparently didn't hold true year round. Juan Maria Osuna told Hayes in October 1870, that *".. it was very cold in the winter"* and that the Indians went down to Guatay Valley and other warm places then.

Chief Jose Cuish-cuish was hereditary chieftain of all Indians in that region in 1870. He was the son of the chieftain who was supposed to have sold Mitaragui to Lassitor and was at Huacupin when Judge Hayes visited in July that year. He was about 45 years old then.

YGUAI: Verifying the location of the site of historic Yguai played a key part in establishing the north boundary of the Rancho Cuyamaca Grant in the famous land dispute of the early 1870s.

The rancheria has had various spellings - Iguai, Iguae, Iguayee and Yguia. The site lies east of the present intersection of Sunrise Highway and State Route 79 and is outside the boundaries of the State Park. At the time Judge Hayes visited it in 1870, the area was a dense forest from the village site west to the top of North Peak. Subsequent cutting of fire wood for the boilers of the Stonewall Mine and fireplaces of the settlers, reduced the forest to bare land.

The village name was also applied to the North Peak by the natives. The Indians called it "E-yee", meaning "Nest" according to Maria Alto. It was applied to the peak because the Indians believed that there was *"a big*

*nest or den... on one of its slopes   in which the wild
animals disappeared when hunted, thus safely evading
pursuit".*

JAMATAYUNE: Out of the various spellings of the
past, there has evolved the present corruption of this old
village's name. It is found on current maps as
Samataguma, located in the little valley just northwest of
the town of Guatay.

The old rancheria of Jamatayune lay among the rocks
on a knoll at the head of the valley. According to Judge
Hayes' notes, *"The Indians lived on the west side of this
pile, having their dance grounds on the east side. The holes
in the rocks, for pounding their acorns into meal, are many
on the west side."*

This rancheria was a principal village of the Cuyamaca
complex. It was noted in the writings of earliest white
men to encounter the people of this region.

The Indians of this village and the neighboring
rancheria of Guatay never became Christians. Hayes
recorded, *"They always burned their dead. A pile of ashes
at hand with fragments of bone and shells intermixed was
interpreted by our guide to have been one of these funeral
pyres."*

When Hayes visited the village, there was a large
basket, three feet high and "of pyramidal shape" placed
in the middle of the pile of rocks. This was the basket
used for storing the acorn bran. The name, Jamatayume
had its origin in the process of making acorn meal
edible. According to Hayes' guide, Chono, <u>jamat</u> ment
"bran" (of the acorn), and <u>ajune</u>, "to gather".

GUATAY: The valley we call Descanso today, was
known to the earliest white settlers as Guatay. Here is
where two well populated Indian villages were situated.

One was called Hum-poo Arrup ma (Whip of the Wind, located in the upper end of the valley, and Pilch oom-wa (White as Ashes) was just west of the Sweetwater River and across from the site of the present commercial center.

These villages of old Guatay valley were once the favorite winter resorts of the Cuyamaca Indians. As soon as the first winter storm threatened and the acorn harvest had been gathered they left their mountain camps for the warmer clime of Guatay.

The natives of Guatay, like those of the entire Cuyamaca area, remained largely independent of mission influence, keeping their ancient religion and customs intact. They were "gentiles unconverted", Hayes noted. The valley was occasionally occupied by both the Presidio and the Mission of San Diego for stock-grazing early in the nineteenth century, when the only permanent settlers were the Indians. They were still very much present in the 1850s and 1860s.

Some fifty Indians were listed as residing there in the 1860 census. But when Judge Hayes passed through ten years later there were only eight jacales, or huts at the old rancheria. Farmers and cattlemen gradually crowded out the old inhabitants.

INAJA: This village was located on the southwest slope of North Peak. Pronounced 'Anaja' by the Indians it meant 'lasting spring' but was referred to as 'Anahuac' by Judge Hayes and early white settlers. When Hayes visited the village in July 1870 there were thirty inhabitants. The spring watered their gardens and the peach trees which were planted from seeds brought from the mission.

The Inaja Indian Reservation was established by executive order signed by President U.S. Grant in 1875.

Land was set aside some two miles west of the village site and originally contained only 240 acres. Subsequent Federal action in 1891 and 1911 enlarged the reservation to the 851 acres which exists today and belongs to the Inaja-Cosmit Diegueno Band. From 1889 to 1916 the Anahuac School District operated a one room school house on the reservation. The school served both the white and Indian children of that area.

While no Indians currently live on these tribal lands, the band's 1991 member role consists of 91.

FATE OF THE LOCAL INDIANS

Even before the great flood of gold prospectors hit the mountains surrounding Julian in 1870, the Indian population had already been severely decimated.

Millions of American natives began to disappear as the white man came to the western world in the 16th and 17th centuries. Most died as their immune systems were overmatched by the diseases Europeans brought with them. The Spaniards didn't intend to wipe out a whole race of people. But smallpox, diphtheria and whooping cough took a horrendous toll on the Indians.

As time went by, those Indians who weren't killed by the white man's diseases were squeezed off their lands. Some were assimilated into society as cheap labor. Some just moved deeper into uninhabited mountains, or other lands holding no attraction for the white man.

Several Government Reservations were established in the late nineteenth century for San Diego County Indians. But only one was set aside in the Cuyamaca Mountains and it was for the Inaja villagers. Which of the others became permanent homes for Cuyamacas is impossible to trace. Over the years there has been a blending of descendants of various tribes and bands on the County's reservations.

3

Early mining

The gold fever that had a contagious grip on northern California since 1849 didn't really infect San Diego County until two decades later. While sporadic panning and primitive mining had uncovered small finds in the back country as early as the eighteenth century, the real gold-rush didn't occur until later. It was triggered on Washington's birthday, 1870 by revelation of rich ore in a mountain valley to be called Julian City.

Actually, indications of gold in the county's back country were recorded as early as November 10, 1602, when Father Antonio de la Ascensión a member of the second Spanish exposition to visit San Diego, went ashore with a party to examine the area. He recorded the following:

"In the sand on this beach there is a great quantity of yellow pyrites, all full of holes, a sure sign that in the neighboring mountains and adjacent to the port there are gold mines; for the water, when it rains, brings it from the mountains.

A legend has grown over the years about the Indians' gold mining activities during the period when they were under the influence of Franciscan Missionaries during the eighteenth century. It gave this version of the scene:

"Indians gave the Padres gold dust in exchange for trinkets, and on inquiry as to its origin, the Padres were told it was obtained far inland, by pounding a certain quartz. The Padres asked to be taken to the site and this was done. They then constructed arrastras and worked the ledge successfully for many years."

Ancient miners' equipment was discovered at the Cleveland Pacific Mine near Escondido where friars were supposed to have mined sizable quantities of gold.

Other reports of early gold mining activity center around Black Mountain east of Rancho Penasquitos. The whites became acquainted with the Indians' mining there, but considered it not worth the trouble to work.

While it was well known in early day San Diego that placers were being worked, it created little excitement. The natives cared little for gold because it could be obtained only by hard work. The few early foreigner settlers saw bigger profits in trading, raising stock and acquiring land. Add to this the policy of the Mission padres to discouraged mining excitement because they viewed such activity as immoral and likely to upset their work, and we can understand why little was made of gold then.

However, such prominent American merchants as Don Able Stearns was known to have traded in gold dust as early as 1836. In that year he shipped 200 ounces valued at $3,200 to a bank in Boston.

The first geological report indicating likelihood of gold in the Julian region was written more than 20 years before any big strikes were made there. It is contained in Dr. C.C. Perry's report made in late 1849 while traveling with the Army's Mexican Boundary Survey party. That fall he made a reconnaissance across the mountains from San Diego to the Colorado Desert. Instead of taking the usual wagon road through San Pasqual, Santa Ysabel, Warner's, San Filipe, Vallecito, and Carrizo Creek, this party took a short cut across the mountains from the Santa Ysabel Valley to San Filipe. This route took them down the Banner grade where Parry recorded the following:

"... the geological formation exhibited along the eastern slope of the mountain range at this point shows a very sensible change, and in place of the usual forms of feldspathic or quartz granite we meet a more prevalent character of micaceous granite, in which the scales of mica are frequently of large size and very confusedly intermixed. With this also occur mica and talcose slates traversed by quartz veins. At this point then, we have an approach to the gold formation, and in the section of country thus limited, exist the fairest prospects of mineral discovery. "

It took another twenty years before gold was found in these quartz veins.

There were other geological and topographical reconnaissances through this part of the country during the 1850s. They were, however, conducted along the regular wagon route through Warner's, and missed the Julian area.

At least two other significant gold quartz mining operations were developed in the region outside the Julian area, and preceded the Julian strike by some twelve years.

In 1857, Judge Oliver S. Witherby developed a mine in the Escondido area. It was noted that in September 1860, he shipped two tons of quartz by boat to San Francisco for crushing since there were no stamp mills in the region. However, by early 1861 the operation was promising enough that Witherby invested in a steam engine and machinery and employed thirty men to operate his mine.

In 1864, the San Diego County assessor listed the Escondido Mining Company as having $2,360 worth of equipment. Newspaper accounts told of Ed Heuck superintendent putting up the first quartz mill in San Diego County on the Rancho Rincon del Diablo, and running an inclined shaft to a depth of 140 feet. The rock averaged $33 a ton and in two years the company took out $30,000. But lack of adequate equipment and sufficient capital forced the mine to close down.

The promise of finding gold and striking it rich in San Diego County mountains was getting considerable attention in the local papers during 1869. Ed Heuck, who was considered something of an expert by then, wrote a piece for the San Diego Union on June 17. He concluded his assessment of the possibilities by saying,

"Persons owning property in the mountains should keep an eye open for the indications and when opportunity offers apply the pick and shovel, and those who are not profitably engaged can do no better than to prospect the North and East of San Diego."

COLEMAN'S DISCOVERY

Whether he was influenced by these accounts or not, A. E. (Fred) Coleman was doing just as Heuck suggested. Coleman lived near Volcan Mountain with an Indian family and herded cattle in Spencer Valley. Late in 1869, he paused at a little creek to let his horse drink, when a glitter of gold in the stream caught his eye. Coleman had worked in the gold fields of northern California and knew what he saw. Wasting no time, he started panning with the skillet he had in his pack.

THE ARESTRA, a primitive quartz mill. When gold was found in its natural condition, in viens of quartz rock, it was necessary to grind it to separate the gold. Mexicans devised a crude machine to do the job, the arestra, which was powered by mule or man. Gold was then readily obtained by washing.

It didn't take long before the word spread, and that little creek was soon crawling with dozens of gold-pan-wielding and sluice-box-shaking fanatics. Reports of how much they were making ranged from two and three dollars a day, to the "twenty dollars a day to the man" that Coleman claimed. While Coleman had a reputation for exaggeration, the number of prospectors grew rapidly, never the less. A settlement of tents and lean-tos was established which they named Emily City, and it was estimated that about seventy-five men were working surface diggings. The Coleman Mining District was formed with Fred being duly elected recorder.

It was at this time and place that the central characters in our developing story of Julian City arrived. Drury Bailey with brothers Frank and James arrived on the scene along with cousins Mike and Webb Julian in late 1869.

Many of the placer miners were naturally trying to trace the origin of the gold, and were working their way up the mountain. It was on February 20, 1870, that Drury Bailey discovered the first quartz ledge which he named the "Warrior's Rest". On the next day, H.C. Bickers, George Gower and J. Bruen Wells discovered the rich quartz which became the Washington Mine.

That was all the evidence the prospectors needed. A meeting was called and the Julian Mining District organized, with Mike Julian named recorder.

As well as discovering the first quartz ledge, Drue stayed on to homestead the site and help establish the thriving mountain town of Julian City.

4
Town Fathers

The Bailey and Julian brothers were Confederate veterans who returned to their homes in Georgia after the Civil War, only to find ruin. With nothing to hold them in Georgia, they made their way west to seek a better life, and eventually found themselves camped in a mountain meadow between the Volcan and Cuyamacas in late 1869.

Post war Georgia presented a bleak landscape of devastation. General Sherman's march to the sea with two great columns, 218 regiments of sixty two thousand men in blue, had cut a swath of destruction fifty miles wide through the heart of the state. Much of the property that didn't fall in the direct path of his troops, was razed and pillaged by "bummers". Burned out plantations, fields growing in weeds, railroads without rolling stock or tracks or bridges was the scene that greeted the returning "Johnny Reb" in 1865.

Michael S. (Mike) Julian was born in 1839, the son of a Forsyth County Georgia farmer who raised Indian corn on 280 acres and owned four slaves. This is the same part of Georgia in which the first United States gold rush occurred at Dahlonega in 1828. It was the center of US gold production for over twenty years and the US government mint was operated there before relinquishing preeminence to the California gold fields and San Francisco in 1850.

It's not known if the Julian family was involved in gold mining in Georgia, but we do know Mike became very much a part of San Diego County's first and only gold rush.

1ST SERGEANT JULIAN

Mike was 22 years old when his native state went to war against the Union. There are four men with Julian surnames listed on army muster rolls in the Georgia State Archives, and all four served in the same unit. They were Robert M., 2d lieutenant; Michael S., 1st sergeant; Alfred W., private and Samuel B., private.

While census rolls for 1850 and 1860 are incomplete and confusing to the researcher, it is believed that three of these men, Michael S. (Mike), Alfred W. (Webb), and Samuel were brothers, while Robert M. was a close cousin.

Robert and Mike enlisted when their company was formed July 22, 1861. Webb enlisted later in November and Samuel the following January. The company was composed of men from Forsyth and Dawson Counties and was called the "Concord Rangers". Edward Smith, a neighbor who lived not far from the Julians, near Concord Churchyard northwest of Comming, signed up 75 volunteers and was elected Captain. Robert Julian was elected 2nd Lieutenant. (In the Confederate Army, all officers below the rank of regimental commander were selected by their men.)

While it appears Georgia Governor Joe Brown encouraged Smith to recruit the company, it turned out the State was unable to support his unit. There were more than enough rebel youngsters clamoring to do battle at the outset of the conflict, but many Confederate states, such as Georgia, were hard pressed to feed, cloth and equip them. North Carolina, on the other hand could produce its own textiles and had ports for blockade-run items, which enabled it to arm and equip units more effectively.

Richmond, the Confederate capital, assigned the "Concord Rangers" to the 2nd Battalion of the North Carolina Infantry, designating them Company D.

What had happened to the Julians' unit is an interesting study in how the Confederate Army was formed in some cases.

Men of political influence were often able to obtain ranks of colonel and general by getting authorization to form and outfit large fighting units. North Carolinian, Colonel Wharton Green was authorized to raise a regiment which was to be part of former Virginia Governor Henry Wise's legion. (Legion was a Confederate term loosely used by volunteer organizations to designate a mixed unit of infantry, cavalry and artillery, slightly larger than a regiment.)

Green, however was able to assemble only five outfitted companies, and three of these were from outside his own state; one from Virginia and two from Georgia. With only five companies, Green was unable to qualify as a regimental commander and had to settle for a battalion. (After the war had been going for three years, and most of the original volunteers had either been taken prisoner or become casualties, the "Concord Rangers" were transferred on April 11, 1864 to the 21st

Regiment, Georgia
Infantry and became
"New Company E". The
reason given was that
the boys should have
been in the Georgia
infantry all along.)

The war record of
the Julian boys was a
checkered one at best.
After many months of
organization and drill,
the battalion was ordered
to engage the enemy for
the first time at Roanoke
Island, North Carolina
in February 1862. The unit
was part of Wise's legion
defending the passage
between Albemarle and
Pamlico Sounds, the
key to Richmond's
back door. But the
Confederates were

no match for General Burnside's 7,500 troops and their
advanced amphibious warfare tactics.

Company D, along with the rest of the 2,700 rebel
troops defending the island were surrendered. Burnside
suffered only 264 casualties in this decisive battle.

The "Concord Rangers" were taken prisoners in their
first battle, before they could get to their positions.
Ten days later they were paroled at Elizabeth City,
however, and released to their homes pending proper

MICHAEL & MARGARET JULIAN met and married in Julian City in 1871. Margaret was the daughter of William Skidmore owner of the Stonewall Mine.

exchange.

Julians' unit existed only on paper for six months until August 18, 1862, when the company was declared exchanged and ordered to reform. In the meantime, they were back home tending to their farms and families. The battalion was reorganized in September 1862 and assigned to Brigadier General Junius Daniel's brigade. Company D reelected the same officers and Mike Julian remained first sergeant.

The battalion was encamped near Richmond for the remainder of 1862 and didn't see action again until February 1863 in Virginia, becoming part of the forces

(Confederate.)	**(Confederate.)**
B 3 Cav. Ga.	B 3 Cav. Ga.
D. D. Bailey	D D Bailey
P.K. , Co. P. , 3 Reg't Georgia Cavalry.	Pvt. , Co. 11. 3 Regiment Georgia Cavalry.
Appears on a	Appears on a
List	**Muster Roll**
of prisoners leaving Cairo, Ill., Oct. 25, 1862, en route for Vicksburg, Miss., for exchange.	of Officers and Men paroled in accordance with the terms of a Military Convention entered into on the 26th day of April, 1865, between General Joseph E. Johnston, Commanding Confederate Army, and Major General W. T. Sherman, Commanding United States Army in North Carolina.
List dated Cairo, Ill., Oct. 25, 1862.	Roll dated *Not Dated*
	Paroled at Charlotte, N. C., May 3, 1865.
Remarks:	Enlisted:
	When *May 13*, 186 2
	Where *Rome Ga*
	By whom *Col Crawford*
	Period *3 ys*
	Last paid:
	By whom *Capt Beriker*
	To what time *Mch 1*, 186 4
	Present or absent
	Remarks:
Indorsement shows: "Rec'd Near Vicksburg on board Steamer Emerald the foregoing Prisoners of War ● ● ● November 1, 1862, from Capt. J. B. Sample, A. A. G. & Agent for exchange of Prisoners. T. J. BEALL, *Lieut. & Agent.*"	
Number of roll:	Number of roll:
3 sheet 7 *J. L. Yent*	34 *A Whealy*
(639b) Copyist.	(639c) Copyist.

PRIVATE DRUE BAILEY was captured at New Haven during the battle of Perryville, Kentucky in early October 1862, but remained a prisoner of war less than three weeks. The muster list (left) shows his unit was exchanged near Vicksburg, free to go back to battle. The muster roll on the right shows he was paroled at the end of the Civil War on May 3, 1895 at Charlotte, N.C.

that held Washington, D.C. under siege in March.

In April, their brigade was ordered to join the Army of Northern Virginia as part of Lt. General Richard Ewell's corps. This took them to Pennsylvania and ultimately into the battle of Gettysburg. There, on July 3, 1863, Mike, Webb and Robert Julian were taken prisoner for the second time. This time, however, they spent considerably more time in POW camps. Mike and Webb, were paroled from Fort Lookout, Maryland in February 1865, while Robert was paroled at Johnson's Island, Ohio in March. Samuel Julian had been discharged in January 1863 as under age and didn't see action at Gettysburg.

CAVALRYMAN DRUE BAILEY

While Julian City was named for another man, it was Drury Dobbins Bailey who homesteaded the land, laid out the town and served as catalyst in its development.

For many years he was a leading spirit in this town he founded. As James Jasper later wrote, he was regarded "as a genial companion and good samaritan, his purse always open at the call of distress."

Drue, as he was called, was born in Dalton, Georgia in 1844. Upon reaching age 18, he too answered the call to arms to fight under the Stars and Bars for his native state.

D.D. Bailey enlisted at Columbus, Georgia as a private in Captain Daniel F. Booton's Company H, 3rd Regiment Georgia Volunteer Cavalry, May 13, 1862. His enlistment, along with his horse, was for "three years or war". The horse was valued at $200 on Company muster rolls. Bailey was paid forty cents a day as a private and was also allowed forty cents a day for "use and risk of horse". Paydays in the Georgia Calvary, however, were

PAY VOUCHER for Confederate Private D.D. Bailey for service from Sept. 1862 to Dec. 1862. During that period he had been taken prisoner in the battle of Perrysville, Ky. and exchanged less than three weeks later. His pay was $12 per month. He was allowed 40 cents a day for "use and risk" of his horse, which apparently he used but 29 days during that three months period.

few and far between.

The 3rd Cavalry Regiment was organized by Colonel M.J. Crawford and mustered into service at Athens, Georgia in early summer 1862. It consisted of men from Rabun, Whitfield and Cherokee counties, the latter being Drue's home.

Crawford's regiment fought under General Joseph Wheeler in the Kentucky campaign of 1862. During the battle of Perryville in early October, Col. Crawford along with 225 officers and men, including Company H with Drue Bailey, were surprised and taken prisoners at New Haven, Ky. For this, Col. Crawford later lost his command.

Muster rolls show they were confined as prisoners of war at Cairo, Illinois but soon after were exchanged aboard the Steamer Emerald near Vicksburg on November 1st. Bailey, Company H and the 3rd Regiment immediately went back to war and later fought in the campaigns of Chickamauga, Chattanooga, Knoxville and Atlanta and were involved in northern Alabama and various conflicts in the Carolinas. After Robert E. Lee's capitulation at Appomattox, the unit was surrendered with the Army of Tennessee on April 26, 1865. Under terms agreed to by U. S. Grant, cavalrymen such as Private Bailey were allowed to keep their horses in order to return home and use them to farm. Unfortunately, there were not too many farms for men like Bailey to return to.

COURIER JAMES BAILEY

James Osborne Bailey, Drue's younger brother and partner in their Ready Relief Mine, was also a Confederate calvary veteran. James joined Company A First Alabama Cavalry at age sixteen in February 1864. The father of the Bailey boys had been driven from their home in Georgia and found temporary refuge in Alabama. James, along with another brother Abijah enlisted in the same company as soon as they were old enough to be inducted.

James' unit was detailed as couriers for Major General Joseph Wheeler's Western Army headquarters. James was known as the 'Boy Courier'. He was small in stature, not weighing over 100 pounds, but muscular and active as an acrobat and was respected by all his comrades for his sense of humor and bravery. His duty as courier took him inside Federal lines. His unit was ultimately surrendered at Greensboro North Carolina on April 5, 1865.

The Federal and Confederate Armies differed in many operational and organizational respects. This in spite of the common background and training their military leaders shared in pre-Civil War service. It should be noted here, that although James Bailey had been recognized by his comrades for extreme bravery on several occasions, there were no medals to show for it when the war was over. The Confederate Army did not bestow awards to their heros as did their opponents. General Lee considered all of his men heros and it wouldn't do to single anyone out. Also, unlike the enlistment of "Billy Yank" that was usually for a set term, ie; one or two years, the standard enlistment for "Johnny Reb" was for "3 years or war".

BAILEY'S HOMESTEAD

Drue Bailey recorded a declaration of homestead on July 30, 1874. It was for the 160 acre site that he named Julian City and which remains as the central part of Julian today. After fourteen years, and many trials and tribulations, including the attempted float of the Cuyamaca Grant boundary over Julian (more about that to follow), Bailey received a homestead patent for 154.65 acres, signed by President Grover Cleveland on June 23, 1888.

In the meantime he donated a portion of the land for both the first grammar and high schools, a lot for a public hall, a lot for the jail, and when approached for a lot for a church, he replied characteristically, *"Sure thing, I'll donate a lot for a church in every block if some*

MR. & MRS. DRURY BAILEY pictured in 1875. Annie Laurie Bailey was the daughter of Drue's mining associate L.B. Redman.

denomination will build on it."

It is said that many a poor miner gladly testified to his generosity, backed by a free deed to a lot upon which he could build a little shack.

Drue Bailey did not confine his gold mining activities to Julian City. The first quartz mine discovery, his Warrior's Rest proved to be only a pocket. Further prospecting led him down the grade to Banner. There, along with brother James and L.B. Redman, a Julian

DRURY D. BAILEY shown at the Redman Mine in 1918, three years before he died at age 77.

assayer, they searched long and hard before finally finding a gold-bearing ledge.

Redman saw the glint of gold under some leaves while picking wild grapes along Chariot creek. The Redman mine was a good one, but not as lucrative as one Drue staked on the same ledge, but across the creek.

Bailey's find came when his funds were almost depleted and he wrote his brother, *"Come at once. I have ready relief."* Thus was born the name of his famous mine - the Ready Relief which made mining history on several occasions. Some of the quartz from this mine yielded as high as $500 per ton while $300 a ton was not uncommon. One selected sample which caused considerable excitement and made mining history yielded $250,000 to the ton.

Drury devised an ingenious overshot water wheel to provide economical power for his stamp mill. Brother James Bailey, who had staked an adjoining claim, ran the Ready Relief mill and processed ore for other Banner mines as well. He was known as one of the few honest operators in the area. He collected only a milling fee for his services while many other stamp mill operators seemed to have trouble "losing' a considerable portion of the miners gold in their processing.

San Diego capitalists bought out Bailey's rich lode in 1874. The Ready Relief was as profitable for the new owners as it had been for its discoverer, but when one of the principal owners died, it provided Drury the opportunity to repurchase the operation, which he did in 1881.

Year after year, the Ready Relief continued to be a consistent producer. During the slump of the 1890s, it was said that "it was the only mine in the district which kept a pick going."

Drury Bailey never patented the Ready Relief nor any other of the ten claims he and his brothers owned in the Banner area. When asked why not, he replied that if he did, he probably would not have worked them, and added that mines had to be worked if they were to pay.

The required assessment work evidently paid off as an incentive. Drury was one of the few original miners who continued to work his claims throughout most of Julian's mining history.

After 30 years of working their mines, the Bailey brothers finally sold their Banner property in 1903 to a syndicate of Boston capitalists for $300,000.

Drury Bailey and Annie Laurie Redman, daughter of Drue's mining associate, were married in 1875. Of their 12 children, nine survived infancy. Drue died in 1921 and Mrs. Bailey in 1927.

MIKE JULIAN'S LATER YEARS

It's been said that the town was named Julian because Drury Bailey, who homesteaded the site and laid it out, said Mike was "handsomer than himself". Perhaps that was one of Bailey's jokes. But actually, it seems, Mike Julian had exhibited leadership qualities throughout his life, and the honor no doubt was bestowed upon him more for his abilities than his appearance.

Beside serving as a first sergeant during the war, Mike started, and was elected recorder for the mining district. When it came time to start a school district, it was Mike who took the lead and was one of the first members of the board of trustees.

He ran for the office of San Diego County Assessor in 1871 and was elected. It was said he didn't care for the job once he got it, serving for one term and deciding not to run for reelection in 1873.

In 1871 Mike Julian met and married an attractive young lady by the name of Margaret Skidmore, daughter of William Skidmore, the discoverer of the Stonewall Mine. They didn't actually live in Julian City long, for after assuming his duties as assessor, he and Margaret found it difficult living far from the county seat and moved into San Diego. They never moved back to the town which was named in his honor.

William Skidmore, Mike's father-in-law, was unable to fully capitalize on his discovery of the Stonewall Mine. It was located on Cuyamaca Grant land and he was forced to sell his claim for a pittance. But being a former mule skinner, he still had the means of his basic livelihood, his mules.

Jonathan Bixby was raising vast fields of grain on his ranch located where north Long Beach now stands and contracted with Skidmore with his 36 mules, to thresh grain. Mike and Margaret Julian moved to Los Nietos Valley, near Downey, to help.

In 1892, after the family had enjoyed several summers camping near the ocean in Long Beach, they decided to make that town their permanent home. Mike saw an opportunity for a new hotel in the town and soon built the Iowa Villa Hotel. In 1897, he built the Julian Hotel, which he sold in 1899. It was later renamed the Lincoln Park Hotel which stood into the 1960s when it became a victim of urban renewal. Mike was to build and operate one more hotel before he died in 1905. It was the Colonial Hotel located just two blocks up Ceder Street from the Julian. Margaret Julian died in Downey in 1931. The couple was survived by three sons, Will, Ray and Ed.

While Mike Julian never moved back to San Diego County, his first return visit to Julian City after an eighteen year absence, caused quite a stir, as reported in the July 30, 1891 edition of the Julian Sentinel. Editor Jasper wrote that having heard Mike just hit town, and in quest of a story: *"We found the object of our search in the postoffice surrounded by friends of long ago. He evidently enjoyed the situation, and it was some time before we were permitted to grasp the hand that felled the first tree and swung the first pick in these hills. After being informed that the fastest town, the fastest horse and the fastest paper in the county bore his name, he remarked: "I have just come in from a camping trip and may look a little rusty, but just rub me a little and you will have the fastest man too."*

The horse Jasper referred to, named "Mike Julian", was bred by James Madison in the late 1880s. In its day, it proved in many match races to be the fastest quarter-horse in the mountains.

THIS STYLISH HOTEL was built and operated by Mike Julian from 1897 until 1899 when he sold it. Named the Julian Hotel, it was located in Long Beach, Calif. on Ceder between Ocean and First Streets. Later renamed the Lincoln Park Hotel, it stood until the 1960s when it fell to urban renewal.

After recounting some of Mike Julian's many accomplishments, Jasper went on to write, *"We encouraged him to play the entertainment act, of which he is certainly a master. We trust he will visit us again shortly, for he possesses a fund of information and romance that we delight to tap."*

5

Dark Cloud

There probably has never been a more troubling chapter in the history of any young town than that which befell Julian City in its infancy.

The boom was no sooner in full swing in the spring of 1870 when a dark cloud descended over that rag-town. It took form as a grab for the mines and the very land upon which the settlers had built their hopes and dreams.

The cloud would hover over the community for three and a half long years causing many miners and settlers to give up. Property with title in dispute couldn't be improved, developed or sold. Most of the miners left for new discoveries in Tombstone, Arizona and many farmers and settlers simply drifted off to other more promising country.

It cost those who stayed and fought considerable anxiety and much of their meager resources.

The villains in the plot were four men who had purchased the 35,500 acre Cuyamaca Rancho from Don

Agustin Olvera. They were Robert Allison, Isaac Hartman, John Treat and Juan Manual Luco, who had bought the grant located south of Julian in 1869, acquiring it for its grazing land and timber resources. Allison had in fact erected a sawmill about four miles south of John Mullkins' Green valley ranch and started logging operations.

But when news started breaking of the discovery of lucrative gold finds in the hills to the north, these men sat up and took notice. Surely they thought, these mines located on land not far from their's were part of their grant -- or should be -- and they set out to claim them.

At least two of the four had gained reputations earlier as scoundrels. This was not the first time they had been involved in attempted landjumping.

Juan Manual Luco was an attorney skilled in land litigation; a man of means who was deft at practicing fraud, forgery, perjury and bribery when necessary to achieve his ends.

Luco was part owner of the ex-Mission Grant and had, just one year earlier, made an unsuccessful run at part of the San Diego Pueblo lands. He attempted to establish that the Pueblo grantees had claimed more land than was allowed under Spanish law, and that the excess should apply to his Mission grant. Luco struck out on that bid.

Furthermore, Luco had presented in 1853 the fraudulent Solono and Yuba County Ulpinos claim to the U. S. Land Commission and Supreme Court. This, according to noted historian H.H. Bancroft, was one of the most carefully prepared of the crooked cases ever to be presented to the land commission. The claim was rejected by mandate as fraudulent throughout, Governor Pio Pico's signature and the government seal being forgeries and testimony on occupancy for the most part perjury.

In another case, however, involving the Milpitas grant in Monterey County, Luco was able to increase the original bounds of his land grant from 12,000 to 30,000 acres to include the lands of some 100 settlers. That was done by presenting a survey which was located without reference to the original bounds and a grant purportedly signed by Governor Alvarado. The signature was later shown to be forged since Alvarado was not even in power when the document was supposed to be signed. The settlers later fought a desperate battle to have this fraud exposed and the wrong redressed, but without success.

John Treat also had a record of questionable land dealings in San Francisco and had attempted to carve out some San Diego Pueblo land by squatting and fencing a parcel.

With this background, it should have been no surprise to anyone who knew these men's past that they might attempt to grab the newly discovered gold fields.

In April 1870, less than two months after the big gold quartz strike at the Washington Mine, they made their move. Claiming their Rancho lines extended over the newborn mining district, they requested Sherman Day, U.S. Surveyor-General for California, to make a Government Survey of the Cuyamaca Grant. Day obliged by assigning the job to Deputy Surveyor James Pascoe. But even before the survey was begun, it became evident that one of the grant owners had influenced the surveyor, as Pascoe stated he intended to establish the northern boundary of the Cuyamaca at the Santa Ysabel Rancho line, which was about two miles north of the mines.

On May 25, 1870, the grant owners called a mass meeting in Julian and more than 500 gathered to hear what they had to say. A deal was offered allowing the miners to continue developing their claims provided royalties were paid them on all ores extracted. The rate schedule for what they referred to as "their Cuyamaca Mines" was as follows: Ores yielding $15 or less per ton would pay $1 per ton (with mining and milling costs estimated at $10 per ton, this amounted to twenty per cent of the net yield); Ores yielding $100 per ton would pay one-third; ores yielding $175 or more would be assessed 50%; the different grades in between would pay a proportionate percentage.

Three days later, in response to miners appeals for help from San Diego, a mass meeting was held at Horton's Hall in New San Diego. Townspeople from Julian and San Diego discussed *"ways and means for the protection of the members of the Julian District and vicinity, in their legal rights, as the attempt now being made by the holders of the Cuyamaca Grant to float their lines over the rich gold mines of the section."*

There were those present who favored calling in "Judge Lynch" to assist. But it was pointed out by cooler heads that hanging the crooks would not get them anywhere, and that the battle had to be fought by legal means. A committee was formed to raise money for what would prove to be a long and costly legal battle. San Diego businessman, Aaron Pauly was elected chairman and J.T. Gower and C.P. Taggart were appointed to confer with the miners. A.E. Horton, W.H. Ogden and Taggart were named to the finance committee. Gower was one of the discoverers of the Washington Mine, Taggart was a San Diego lawyer and Horton has been referred to as the "father of New San Diego".

On June 9th, the San Diego Union reported that Pascoe had gone into the mountains to run the lines, accompanied by John Treat and a bevy of surveyors.

About this time Pauly visited the gold region along with a lawyer he had engaged named George Yale. Yale told the miners to relax and go back to work. "The fraud," he said "was too plain to stand for a moment in the light of legal investigation." This considerably raised the miners spirits making them feel confident quick work could be made of those land-grabbers. What many of them didn't fully appreciate was the tenaciouness of the rapscallions they were facing.

Wiser heads in San Diego such as Major L. Chase and Ephraim W. Morse, however, disagreed with Yale. They cautioned the miners that the only way they could win was to produce proof - hard evidence showing where the grant boundaries actually were located.

While Yale was suggesting the settlers take the case to the U.S. Supreme Court, another attorney had started spade-work on a case that would ultimately carry the miners to victory. He was the renowned Judge Benjamin Hayes.

It was the Interior Department - their Surveyor General and Land Commissioner who passed on surveys and would have the say, not the Supreme Court. Hayes took to the field with diseno and notebook intent on finding and verifying key locations shown on the Mexican grant map (diseño) - the key document that would ultimately determine the outcome in the dispute. For the better part of July, 1870 Hayes, Samuel Ames and Indian guide Chono visited with settlers and Indians throughout the country, from the assistencia at Santa Ysabel, south through the Cuyamaca mountains to Descanso and Viejas. Samuel Ames had carried mail and passengers for Birch's "Jack-Ass Mail" through that area during the late 1850s. He had also been a partner with John Mulkins, farming Green Valley during the 1860s, and knew the Cuyamacas well.

Apparently Hayes had either taken it upon himself to start this work, or was retained in anticipation of Yale's departure. In any event, it developed by year's end Gregory Yale's name had been dropped from all items concerning the dispute and Hayes was listed as the miner's attorney effective January 1, 1871.

Notices of Pascoe's survey were published according to law in October 1870, which allowed ninety days for filing objections. On January 2nd, Hayes was prepared and filed formal exceptions to the Pascoe survey. His filing contained approximately thirty supporting affidavits and exhibits. The objections stated that Pascoe's survey *"includes lands which are beyond the exterior limits of said rancho, and to which land exceptants (miners and settlers) are entitled."* It was also noted that the grant boundary should be no further north than the most northerly of the three Cuyamaca peaks.

BENJAMIN IGNATIUS HAYES

It would be timely to insert a note here about Judge Benjamin I. Hayes. While he was never a resident of Julian or vicinity, he played a major role in the history of that area - as well he did, in many other parts of southern California.

Hayes was born in Maryland in 1815, graduated from St. Mary's College, Baltimore and was admitted to the Maryland bar at the young age of 24. He soon after moved to Missouri practicing law in Liberty then on to St. Louis where he went into partnership with two associates in the publication of a temperance journal.

The California gold rush of 1849 beckoned and he left to seek his fortune, arriving in Los Angeles in early 1850. Apparently the opportunities seemed better there than in the gold fields. California was soon to be admitted as a state and new counties were being formed and were electing their first officials. On April 1, 1850 he was elected to be the first Los Angeles County Attorney. At that same election, Don Agustin Olvera was elected Los Angeles County's first judge.

It's little wonder Hayes knew as much as he did about the old Mexican regime. For this first election of L.A. County officials, a secret junta of prominent Angelinos had met in early March at the home of Olvera, a lawyer who played a lead role in bridging the gap between California's Mexican and American days. A slate of candidates, dominated by Californios, was drawn for these first County offices and it won by a large majority. The winners took office the same day they were elected.

After getting settled, Hayes sent for his wife, Emily Chauncey whom he'd married shortly before leaving for California.

In 1852, Hayes was elected the first Judge of the Southern District of California which included Los Angeles, San Bernardino and San Diego Counties. He held that office until 1864 when he was defeated for reelection by Pedro de la Guerra who had made a speech in the State Senate on a bill that threatened Mexican claims, and had a great effect in electing him over Hayes.

Judge Hayes spent many of his later years in Old Town San Diego, representing San Diego County in the state assembly from 1865 to 1867.

By 1870 he had gained the reputation as the best informed man in the state on grant titles, thus commending him for the tough job of fighting the attempted grab for the mines.

Hayes died in Los Angeles in 1877 at age 62. His son J. Chauncey settled in Oceanside and raised a large family. Many of Hayes' decendents still reside in that area.

HAYES' NOTES

While Hayes was investigating and taking careful notes on the various sites shown on Olvera's diseño for the Julian settlers' case, he was at the same time adding valuable written information to the bank of history about the natives who occupied the Cuyamaca mountains. He pin-pointed the location of early Indian villages, trade routes and pioneer trails. He was also a noted collector of numerous volumns of scraps of information on early California. *"His patience and forethought in saving these helps to the historian has proved invaluable"* so said H.H. Bancroft, who also noted, *"He was pure-hearted and high-minded in every respect."*

In early July 1870, the Defense League hired civil engineer Charles J. Fox to make a survey of the Cuyamaca Grant. Fox's survey was finished in a few weeks, finding that the Julian mines were a good six miles north of the grant.

Hiring professional help cost money, and before the battle would utimately be resolved several lawyers would be involved and a lot of money would be spent. While the San Diego supporters were organizing support for the miners, the Julianites appointed a committee to take charge of protesting Pascoe's survey. Composed of Colonel L.B. Hopkins, Chester Gunn and William Hammill they were empowered to secure testimony. They also were given "full power to assess all the mines and property in the the Julian, Coleman and Hensley Districts for the purposes of raising funds to carry on the cause to final termination, and to employ attorneys to conduct the same.

The local committee was empowered to assess the various mine and land owners, but there also were other ways the town got together to raise funds. In one case, Mrs Kate Snyder baked a cake to be auctioned off at a dance staged by the Julian City women. Proceeds to go to the Defense fund. Each successful bidder returned the cake to the doner who continued to action it again and again until $75 was raised.

A few weeks later the Banner women gave a dance and also put up a cake for auction to benefit the cause. The Julian miners boasted they would bring that cake to Julian, but the Chariot miners said the cake would stay in Banner. The bidding was brisk. The Chariot miners were successful in their bidding until finally a Julian man got the upper hand. He at once started on the run for the Julian trail with cake in arms and Chariot sprinters at his heels. In turning a sharp corner, the Julianite stumbled over a wash tub, sprawling on top of the cake and turning it into a mass of ruin. This cake had already brought the Defense fund the sum of $175 - a tribute to the donor and the sporting spirit of the miners.

How was it that the grant owners felt they had a good chance of making their grab work? The answer lies in the vague and casual manner in which the typical Mexican land grant boundaries were described and recorded. They also felt thay could successfully exploit a statement made by J. Joaquin Ortega twenty five years earlier when Governor Pio Pico was considering the grant for Agustin Olvera. Ortega had written in 1846:

"The tract known by the name of Cuyamaca is in the vicinity of, or bordering on (colindante con) Santa Ysabel, and is absolutely vacant, and extends to Milquattay and part of the Valle de las Viejas."

The land grant made by Governor Pico to Olvera in 1845, however, was for eight square leagues of land, or

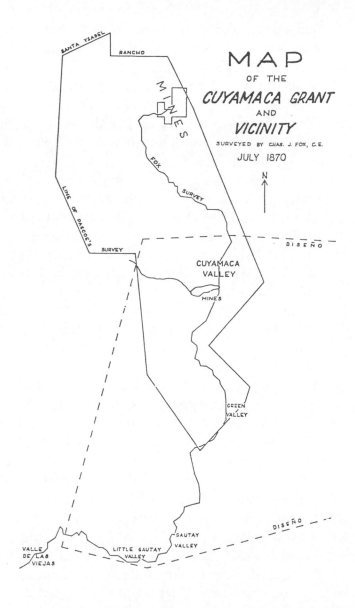

MAP
OF THE
CUYAMACA GRANT
AND
VICINITY
SURVEYED BY CHAS. J. FOX, C.E.
JULY 1870

MEXICAN LAND GRANT MAP, or diseno (opposite), used to establish boundaries of the 35,500 acre Cuyamaca Rancho for Don Agustin Olvera in 1845. Comparing this with the 1870 Fox/Pascoe map (above) reveals how outlandish the attempted "boundary float" really was.

BENJAMIN I. HAYES, lawyer, judge and historian. One who probably did more than any other single person to save the land for the Julian settlers in the early 1870s.

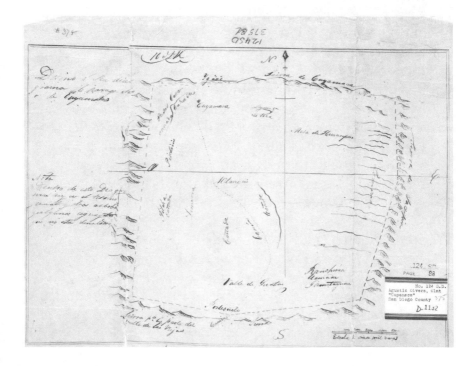

approximately 35,500 acres. Stretching a grant all the way from Valle de las Viejas north to the Santa Ysabel rancho boundary would, however, take in at least twelve to thirteen square leagues. Obviously Pascoe had to start on the north end, at the Santa Ysabel line, and work south if he was to get the gold fields into the Cuyamaca Grant, and at the same time stay within the eight league limit. That apparently is what Treat and cohorts were able to convince Pascoe to do.

HAYES FILING GETS DESIRED RESULTS

Surveyor General J.R. Hardenbergh, the man who had succeeded Sherman Day in February 1871, closed the case for evidence on April 5, 1871. Shortly thereafter he ruled in favor of the miners, disapproving Pascoe's survey. He based his decision on the answers to two questions. First, did the diseno show the tract correctly and could it be identified from the names and topography on it? And secondly, had Pascoe's survey been made within the diseno's boundaries?

Hardenbergh determined that the Fox map was an accurate survey and matched very favorably with the map of the grant made in 1845-6. He noted that the Pascoe map and the Fox map agreed on the location of the Laguna Seca (Cuyamaca Lake today), the Cuyamaca Peaks, the Canada Cascar, Mulkins' house in Green valley, and as to the general direction of the road approximately, and he concluded:

"Admitting the survey of Fox to have been correctly made, I think the foregoing comparison clearly shows that the greater portion of Pascoe's survey is north of the northern boundary of the diseno, and embraces land not included in the same"

The grant owners continued to plead that their land adjoined the Santa Ysabel Rancho based on Joaquin Ortega's 1845 report. But Ortega's report was not mentioned in Pio Pico's grant to Olvera and was not a part of the decree of confimation. Besides, Hayes contended, the words "colindante con" were vague and indefinite and were used to designate neighboring as well as coterminous lands.

In agreeing with Hayes' arguements, Hardenbergh ruled that the diseño was the key to the grant and superior to any report found in the proceedings prior to the issuance of the grant. It was "the controlling locative paper".

Upon news of the decision, the San Diego Union ran the following in their April 29, 1871 edition headed "WELCOME NEWS":

> *"The very welcome intelligence has been received that Pascoe's survey of the Rancho Cuyamaca has been rejected in the office of the Surveyor-General. This is beyond question the most gratifying news that has reached San Diego since the announcement of the passage of the Railroad Bill . . . "*

While most everyone on the miner's side thought the battle was finally over and won, one San Diego pragmatist was not so optimistic. E.W. Morse had written on April 20, 1871 to his friend Amos Weed in Julian:

> *"I think the miners and others opposed to the grant will get tired of law and allow the swindling grant claimants to have their own way, before long. You have already been sold out by your San Francisco lawyer, and you have the most unscrupulous set of blackmailers in the State opposed to you, men who have made it a regular business to purchase these swindling claims, and carrying*

them through the courts by bribes and all kinds of corruption."

Sure enough, the saga was not finished. The case papers and evidence had been forwarded to the Land Commissioner in Washington in October 1871. But final action on such matters usually took a long time. And before the Commissioner got around to taking such action, John Treat got the whole matter reopened again by filing an affidavit on June 7, 1872 claiming irregularities in the way the Surveyor-General handled the case.

CASE REOPENED

On August 21, 1872, sixteen months after the miners had celebrated victory, Land Commissioner Willis Drummond ordered the Surveyor-General to re-examine and re-investigate the case. Apparently the Commissioner agreed with Treat that certain interested parties had not been notified of testimony given; that testimony had not been taken under oath; that opportunity for cross-examination had not been afforded and that evidence of witnesses' character had not been produced at the time Judge Hayes filed his exceptions in January 1871.

The whole process of taking testimony had to be started again in December 1872, under rules set down by the Land Commissioner in Washington.

A new wave of dispair washed over the community. But there were a few indomitable spirits in the camp, such as James Kelley owner of Owens Mine, Drue Bailey of the Ready Relief and George V. King of the Chariot Mines who refused to give up without a fight. Whenever things looked dark, and another set-back loomed, these men would continue to rally the community behind the cause.

This new chapter in the continuing saga of the attempted 'Julian Land Grab' took from November 25, 1872 until April 25, 1873.

For this, and what was most likely to be the last round in the fight, the grant owners brought in a new heavyweight. Their first and major witness was John J. Warner, rancher and owner of Warner's Ranch. Under oath he claimed to have seen the original diseno within the last half year and further stated that he had drawn it up himself:

"I believe all the writing upon it (except that on the left hand margin), is in my handwriting . . . . A dotted line, in a northerly and southerly direction, on the diseño, and marked "camino' (road) was made by myself."

Claiming to have drawn the map at Estudillo's house in San Diego in 1846, he testified that the northern grant boundary was always understood to adjoin the Santa Ysabel Rancho. He admitted under questioning, however, that others must have drawn in the mountains on the diseno, as he had little knowledge of the area having visited the tract but once.

The results of this new hearing were sent back to Washington in June 1873 for the review and action by the Land Commissioner at the Interior Department. Meanwhile, signals reaching the grant owners were not encouraging. Surveyor-General Hardenbergh in San Francisco, was adhering to his former position of denial of the Pascoe survey, and the grantees decided to apply more pressure. They began negotiating separate deals with individual miners and settlers, granting deeds to parcels located on the contested land. The community reacted at a public meeting in Julian on March 16, 1873, denouncing those people who had accepted deeds, declaring they have acknowledged the grantee's claim to the land and placed themselves antagonistic to the welfare of the District, *"the same as if they had joined hands with the grantees in wresting from us our homes and property under a trumped up swindling Spanish grant."*

They warned that such colaborators would either stop such activity or be summarily ejected from the District. There appears to be no record of anyone being punished on this account.

Another ploy used by the grantees during the final rounds of the legal battle was to threaten to bring suit in U.S. Circuit Court against the residents of Julian to prohibit them from cutting wood. They claimed the natural resources of the land were being diminished as the outcome of the case was still pending. Fortunately, the whole issue was resolved before the weather got too severe, with news of the settler's victory.

The miners had retained Washington, D.C. attorney A. St. Clair Denver to present their case before the Commissioner at the Department of Interior during the summer of 1873. It was Denver whose job it was to present the evidence gathered by Hayes, and to challenge the grant owner's presentations.

At long last, on November 29, 1873 the San Diego Union received a telegram from J.B. Lang, of the Golden Chariot Mine, who was then in San Francisco.

"Pascoe's survey of the Cuyamaca Grant is rejected by Commissioner Drummond. Dispatch news to Julian immediately." The mining town went wild with the news. Salutes were given by firing Giant powder cartridges, anvils, and anything else that would make a loud noise.

The Julian correspondent for the San Diego Union reported the feelings of the people:

"To say we are glad hardly expresses it. We feel as if a great load had been lifted; the cloud that has been

hanging over us burst; -- we are now the owners of our mines, our farms, and our homes."

Drummond's official report denying the Pascoe survey was not printed until January 1874; the official land patent was not drawn along the lines of the Olvera diseño until November 14, 1974; and the patent to the grant, now containing 35,501.32 acres, was not signed by President U.S. Grant until December 19, 1874. The wheels of justice did indeed grind exceedingly slow, but justice did prevail.

After three and a half years of a battle that ebbed and flowed, the people of Julian finally won the right to keep their land. Luco and his partners had to content themselves with only those gold mines located within the legitimate grant boundary firmly established well south of the town of Julian. As it later proved, ironically, the richest mine in that whole mountain area was the Stonewall Mine which was indeed located within the Cuyamaca Grant.

Juan Luco undoubtedly was the instigator of the attempted land grab at the outset. In reviewing newspaper accounts of the period, it is obvious he stayed in the background and let his partners do the talking. As a result, the main villain in the settler's eyes was John Treat, who seemed to be the local point man for the partners. It was Treat who brought down the wrath of the community and who was actually hung in effigy before the whole matter was laid to rest. (A very long poem detailing the land-grab saga was published in the San Diego Union in December 1873. It refers to the hanging. The poem can be found as Appendix B, in its entirety.)

Confusion over who owned what within the final boundaries of the rancho was settled by court appointed referees in 1879. John Treat stayed in the area and

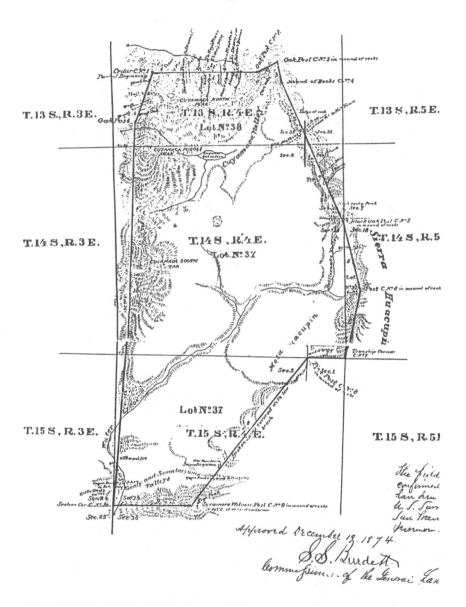

APPROVED SURVEY finally established Cuyamaca Rancho boundaries in December 1874. This allowed settlers outside the grant to homestead "open Government land". Until this survey was approved, farmers and miners who had settled nearby were gambling on being able to perfect title to their land.

subsequently developed a very successful dairy operation on the 1,231 acres he retained in the northwest part of the grant. Known as the Milk Ranch, the dairy is said to have supported as many as 1,000 pure bred Jerseys and produced as much as 10,000 pounds of butter in a year.

Robert Allison also remained. He retained 3,500 acres of Rancho land in the Guatay Valley. It is said he raised as many as 700 sheep and in one year produced 800 tons of hay on 500 acres.

Luco realized about 2,600 acres after the rancho land was divided, but there's no record of his settling there.

CUYAMACA GRANT BACKGROUND

The country we think of today as Cuyamaca, extends from the Guatay Valley in the south, to Cuyamaca's North Peak. The original Mexican grant boundary had pretty much defined it that way.

The Cuyamaca Rancho was first obtained by Agustin Olvera by grant from Mexico's last California territorial governor, Pio Pico.

Don Augustin was a prominent member of the close-knit Mexican Californio establishment. In 1845, the year he filed an expediente for the Cuyamaca, he was secretary of the ruling Departmental Assembly. He had already been granted the Rancho Mission Vieja , three leagues of land in San Juan Capistrano.

The name Olvera is popularly associated today with that Los Angeles street and tourist attraction bearing his name. It was on that street that he lived and practiced law for many years. Olvera later became one of Los Angeles' first judges under American rule.

When Olvera petitioned for the Cuyamaca, he hadn't any personal knowledge of the land. It was just another God-foresaken, out of the way place in the mountains sixteen leagues east of San Diego. He simply saw an opportunity to obtain some grazing and timber land.

Before he would take possession, however, there were certain prerequisites and formalities required under Mexican law. A diseño (map) had to be prepared that matched the features and measure of the requested land.

When he petitioned Gov. Pico on June 5, 1845 he said he would present a proper diseno in due time but was prevented from doing so at the moment because of duties of his office.

While the law was clear, often times it was not strictly adhered to. In many respects, California governors had been careless in granting lands. There was one instance wherein Gov. Micheltorena ordered that every person in the Northern District of Califronia, who had petitioned for land before a certain date, and whose petition had not been acted upon, should be the owner of that land, provided the nearest Alcalde should certify that it belonged to the public domain.

The first white man of record to try to settle on this land didn't arrive until after Olvera had nailed down the grant from Pio Pico. He was Cesario Walker and he agreed in 1847 to set up a saw mill and cut timber for the new owner.

Olvera saw an opportunity to make some money since lumber being imported from northern California at the time was selling for $50. per thousand board feet. Walker started the operation, but he didn't last long, being scared off by the Indians. Hostilities between American and Mexican forces were heating up and the Indians saw this as a good time to make it difficult for white settlers attempting to preempt their lands.

It should be noted that even by 1870, some 20 years after California had become part of the United States, much of San Diego County had yet to be officially surveyed and those surveys certified by the new government. U.S. Surveyor General crews had finished work on the San Vicente Rancho boundary in December 1869 and were at work on the Santa Maria and Santa Ysabel ranchos in early 1870. Boundary surveys of the various confirmed Mexican grants had to be done before the federal government could determine that the balance of land was open and available for homestead. This left many pioneers who settled near such ranchos in a tenuous position. Farmers, cattlemen and miners alike, were in the same boat. Until the official surveys were certified, many of them were gambling they had staked out and invested their hard labor in land which could some day be patented as homesteads in their names.

The news that Pascoe's phony survey had finally and positively been rejected, and that a new survey would follow the boundaries of the Mexican disneo, represented the most important first step for the settler seeking a homestead. Knowing they were firmly on 'Government Land' ment their gamble had paid off. No wonder the great relief and celebration on that momentous day in November 1873.

MORTAR AND PESTLE used to break up small quantities of gold bearing quartz. Once the quartz was ground, the gold was easier to recover, usually by washing with water. Shown next to it is a small mold used to form ingots.

6

After the Rush

By 1876, most of the easily recovered gold had been recovered. For the next decade nearly all the mines lay dormant. The population of Julian dropped to 100 and in 1881 the Julian and Banner mining districts were combined into the Julian District.

Over the years, Julian gold production has mostly been a boom or bust affair. Mines would close down over some problem or difficulty, then reopen when things got better. Except for a few mines, the business of taking gold from the mountains around Julian, was not especially lucrative. When compared with the wealth that came out of the Klondike, or the Mother Lode country of northern California, Julian's total production of about five million dollars was a drop in the bucket. *"To be sure, it was not so much as gold rushes go."* one scholar later wrote, *"But whatever its size, it left its imprint upon the countryside. And it was the best gold rush Julian ever had."*

By 1913, the Julian Mining District, which then included Banner, listed 73 recorded mining claims. Of these, 14 were patented. Some had paid their owners a respectable return. Most didn't.

With the coming of the great depression in the early 1930s, there was a marked increase in gold mining activities in the back country. The once lucrative mines of Julian and Banner got a second look, and some even began paying their owners small returns when worked in a limited way. From 1923 to 1933 nearly $43,000 was taken out of the Julian district, with ten percent of that coming from placers.

On July 6, 1933, the Julian Mining District, that had been formed by Mike Julian 63 years earlier, officially came to an end. The complete records were taken over by the San Diego County Recorder.

During the late 1930s there was a great deal of talking, big planning and wishful thinking, but relatively little action in the way of mining. With World War II came good jobs and gold mining in San Diego County came to a halt for lack of workers. Following the war the "big planners" returned but again very little actual mining took place. County production figures showed a mere $70 in 1946, $455 in 1947 and by 1949 recorded production had dropped to but three ounces worth $105.

The fixed price of $34.91 per ounce of gold established by the federal government in 1934 made it impossible to recover gold profitably in relation to high production costs. Even today, with the price of gold freed, there are few places in the world that can produce gold profitably, and Julian certainly is not one of those.

In 1934, the California Division of Mines summed up 63 years of mining and estimated that total gold production for the Julian - Banner - Cuyamaca region was between $4,000,000 to $5,000,000.

The largest producers were:

Stonewall	$2,000,000
Golden Chariot	700,000
Ready Relief	500,000
Helvetia	450,000
Owens	450,000
Blue Hill or Gardiner	200,000
North Hubbard	200,000
Ranchita	150,000

The following were estimated as producing between $25,000 and $50,000 each:

Antelope	Madden
Chaparral	Redman
Cincinnati Bell	San Diego
Eagle	Shamrock
Elvado	Van Wert
Hidden Treasure	Warlock
High Peak	Washington
Kentuck S.	

Producers of less than $25,000 in gold were:

Cable	Homestake
Chieftain	Neptune
Eldorado	North Star
Ella	Oriflamme
Fraction	Padlock
Gold King	Ruby
Gold Queen	South Hubbard
Granite Mountain	Tom Scott

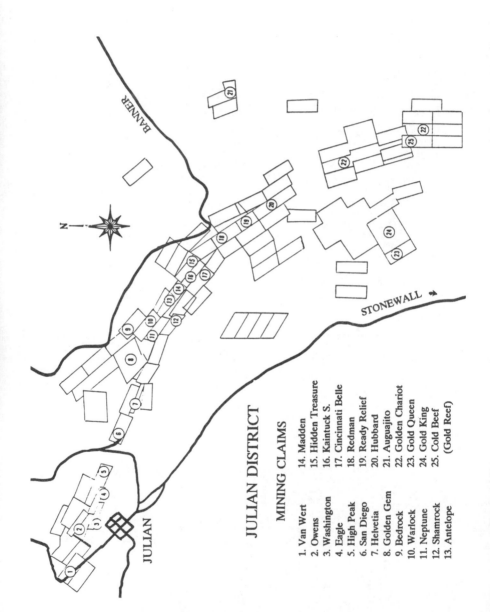

JULIAN DISTRICT

MINING CLAIMS

1. Van Wert
2. Owens
3. Washington
4. Eagle
5. High Peak
6. San Diego
7. Helvetia
8. Golden Gem
9. Bedrock
10. Warlock
11. Neptune
12. Shamrock
13. Antelope
14. Madden
15. Hidden Treasure
16. Kaintuck S.
17. Cincinnati Belle
18. Redman
19. Ready Relief
20. Hubbard
21. Auguajito
22. Golden Chariot
23. Gold Queen
24. Gold King
25. Cold Beef
    (Gold Reef)

From the standpoint of historical interest several operations are noteworthy.

THE WASHINGTON was the first quartz strike of importance in Julian and set off the gold rush of 1870. It was discovered by H.C. Bickers who had extensive experience as a miner and mill man. He had worked in the California and Idaho gold fields before drifting to San Diego County.

While following the tracks of a bear up a ravine, just north of the present Julian townsite, Bickers stumbled upon some gold-bearing quartz. He showed it to his companions J. Bruen Wells, a preacher, and George Gower, a surveyor who had just completed work on the San Vicente Grant boundary survey. (Gower Mountain located on the north edge of San Vicente Valley is a prominent topographical feature he named for himself while working in that area in the winter of 1869.)

Wells refused even to look at the specimen because it was Sunday. The following day was Monday and Washington's birthday so they christened the mine the George Washington and their camp Mount Vernon.

Word of the discovery spread fast and men came from every direction looking for extensions. But the discoverers first managed to write down the names of 21 relatives as co-claimants and established their right to 4,200 feet of space on the quartz ledge.

Within a few weeks Bickers and Gower took nearly a ton of their rich ore to San Diego on muleback where 400 pounds of it was displayed in a store on 5th Avenue. Gower took the remaining ore to San Francisco by steamer and sold it for $500. The partners didn't see any of the money, however. It melted away with the bright lights of The City and Gower's high spirits.

The Washington was never one of the biggest

producers in the area, but it did pay its owners a respectable return for their work and investment.

The Julian Historical Society owns the mine today and maintains a mining equipment exhibit for the interested visitor.

THE OWENS This mine joined the Washington on the north and was claimed about a month later. Discovered by Barney Owens and James Kelly it became a very profitable operation. It made money for several different owners over the years. As recently as 1940, money was being invested in the mine in hopes of more production. At present, it has been bulldozed shut to prevent accidents.

EAGLE-HIGH PEAK These two mines were registered in the spring of 1870 and join underground. Located on "Gold Hill", a short drive north of Julian town center, this operation is open to the public every day and is a very popular tourist attraction. There is a blacksmith shop and a museum with old mining equipment.

These two mines produced between $25,000 and $50,000 in gold each. But mining operations ceased in 1907 after a tragic accident took the lives of the superintendent and another miner.

The operation looks very much as it did ninety years ago and the public is welcome to take a guided walk through its mountain tunnels.

THE HELVETIA Ranking high on the Julian list of mines for total gold production, the Helevetia was discovered in August 1870. It is located one mile east of Julian on the southwest side of the old Banner Grade. Plagued by accidents and legal difficulties, the operation was shut down and started up again on several occasions.

Some experts believe the mine is still capable of yielding a good profit, but today it lies idle and deserted.

THE WARLOCK Another mine that was one of the first to be discovered and was still being worked into the mid-20th century. Located about two miles east of Julian, the Warlock intersected seven veins, including the Bedrock, Kentuck S., Cincinnati and the Shamrock. In 1962 the mine was declared a radioactive fallout shelter for 222 persons. Civil Defense authorities stored food, water and medical supplies in the mine shaft, but had to give up on the shelter due to pilferage and a cave-in that rendered it unusable.

THE GOLDEN CHARIOT was the all-time second best producing gold mine in the region. It was discovered by a destitute George Valentine King in early 1871. Like many another lucky strike, the rich ore was accidently discovered when the weary, day-dreaming prospector broke off a piece of quartz from the rock he was sitting on and was awe struck at seeing it sparkle in the sunlight. His partners and he staked out a 1,200 foot long and 200 foot wide claim and named it the Golden Chariot.

Despite their rich ore, the owners had no money to buy mining equipment at first. Yet each managed to hack out enough gold with picks, hammers, mortars and pestles to net four or five dollars a day.

The trail to the mine was so rugged that it took a small fortune, for those days, to build a wagon road to get the rich ore out. But a good road was a necessity if the mine's potential was to be realized. Joe Swycaffer contracted with the owners to do the job for $1,790.

The mine prospered and King was able to sell his one-quarter interest to his other partners for $25,000, less than two years after he discovered it.

The Golden Chariot was sold to San Francisco capitalists at the end of 1873 for $96,000 gold coin. While it made its new owners a handsome profit, the mine played out by 1875 and was shut down.

THE RANCHITA was the last of the area's major mines to be discovered. It is located on the west side of a spur of Granite Mountain which forms a side of the grade from Banner to San Felipe Valley.

It was discovered in the summer of 1895 by Leandro Woods, a young cowboy working on the Lopez homestead, a short distance from their ranch house. Woods worked the mine himself and when he had accumulated two or three thousand dollars in gold he'd throw a big party. Renting a suite at the Hotel del Coronado he invited many friends to enjoy his hospitality. When the money ran out, he went back to the mine to start all over again.

But this lasted only a few months. In the fall of 1895, Woods sold the mine to Cave J. Couts, Jr. son of the well-known pioneer, for $5,500 cash. Couts contracted with others to operate the mine which resulted in mismanagement and litigation.

While the Ranchita was considered to have more potential than most of the neighboring mines, it's believed the operation never was worked to that potential.

Other historically interesting mines include the Banner, Ready Relief and Stonewall which are mentioned in other chapters of this book.

7

Trail and Transport

Before gold was discovered in Julian in 1870, wagon roads through San Diego County followed the well worn path of migration into California. There wasn't much need to haul heavy goods and people into the mountains, so roads for wheeled vehicles in the Cuyamacas were non-existent.

Pioneers who settled the back country during the 1850s relied on a few tried and true routes to freight in their needs from San Diego and San Bernardino. The earliest settlers of Ballena and Santa Ysabel, such as Sam and Bill Warnock and Dr. George McKinstry used what they called the "Government Highway". From Old Town San Diego, it started by way of the Mission Valley Grade, up Murray Canyon, across the mesa near Camp Kearny, down a canyon into Poway Valley (spelled Paguay then), then north generally following the route we call Pomerado Road today, out the north end to Bernardo Station and up into Highland Valley, overlooking San Pasqual. From there they crossed the Santa Maria

Valley where Ramona is today and followed a course taking them along what we presently call the Old Julian Road. This ran through the Ballena Valley to the old Santa Ysabel Asistencia where it turned north to Warner's Ranch.

Warner's marked the spot where this road from San Diego met the emigrant trail, later called the overland stage route, which came in from the parched desertland to the southeast. Those travelers venturing to San Diego turned south here, while those going on to Los Angeles and San Francisco bore north to Oak Grove and Temecula.

Bill Warnock drove a wagon from his farm in Ballena once a year along this route to San Bernardino. There he stocked up on staples such as flour, beans (if he hadn't raised enough that year), matches, denim cloth and the like. While this road north to San Bernardino was rough, hazardous and time consuming, it was still easier than the route south to San Diego. Besides, Old Town had very little to offer the consumer of the 1850s and 60s.

BUTTERFIELD STAGE

The famed Butterfield stages rumbled through San Diego's desert for several years prior to the eruption of the Civil War. They carried mail and passengers over 2,730 miles of baren and hostile country between Tipton, Missouri and San Francisco, California, making the journey in 24 days.

And *"What"* you ask, *"had Cuyamaca country to do with the legendary Butterfield Stages? Their route did not go through those mountains."* But what some people don't know is that Green Valley, and the ancient Indian trail crossing it, did play an important role in serving and sustaining two vital links in the Butterfield system as well as supporting another overland mail company.

It was in 1857 that John Rule Lassitor, with the help of his step-son John Mulkins, built a crude house at the confluence of Cold Creek and the Sweetwater River and started farming the long Green Valley that splits today's Cuyamaca Rancho State Park. That house was built but a few hundred feet from the present park headquarters.

Lassitor also built the adobe at Vallecito and operated that stage station in the desert far below the Laguna Mountains.

It was from his Green Valley farm that hay came to sustain the horses and the mules needed to carry the early scheduled overland mails.

Lassitor hauled hay by sled and wagon down mountain trails out of Cuyamaca Valley, through Oriflamme Canyon and Mason Valley to his Vallecito Station, as

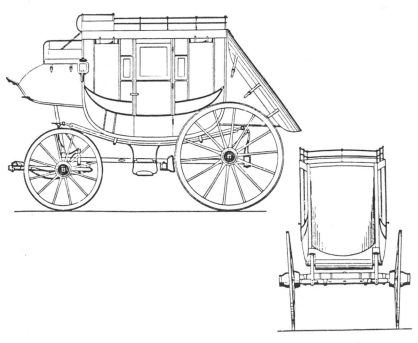

well as to the Carrizo Station further to the south. Sleds were used on the precipitous "Hay Road" snaking east out of the mountains. Wagons couldn't be controlled on such a steep grade.

Vallecito fed and curried strings of horses, supplying the Butterfield system with fresh horsepower for the runs between San Felipe to the north and Carrizo station to the south. Each link between stations in the Butterfield system ran approximately 18 miles.

As the stages braked to a stop in a cloud of dust, the station operator would unharness six lathered steeds and harness six fresh ones, while passengers had some time to stretch, and if it was meal time, catch a bite to eat.

Green Valley also provided feed and a resting place for two other mail services using the ancient Indian trails that wound through desert and mountains.

THE ARMY AND THE JACK-ASS MAIL

There was the Army's Yuma-San Diego mail which was carried from 1853 to 1855. Also the San Antonio & San Diego Mail Line otherwise known as Birch's Overland Mail which ran from 1857 to 1860. Instead of following the emigrant trail to Warner's, then back south to San Diego, these two took the more direct route through the Cuyamacas.

Birch left his stages at Fort Yuma in favor of mules to negotiate the rugged trails. The term "Jackass Mail" was first applied to the Birch operation in 1857 by a taunting San Francisco editor, and used ever since. But a mule is no jackass, as any skinner will testify and while the term was catchy, it was a misnomer.

This route came up from Carrizo Creek to Vallecito, then to the mouth of Canebrake Canon where good water was found at Palm Springs (not Palmitas Spring).

JAMES RULER LASSITOR settled at Vallecito in 1854 and built the sod house that later became the famed Butterfield station. Assisted by his two step sons, John and Andrew Mulkins, he also established a home and farm in Green Valley. He supplied the stage line with hay, hauling it on sleds out of the Cuyamacas down steep trails to the desert. He was a Justice of the Peace in the Cuyamacas and a San Diego County Supervisor in 1862. Lassitor was murdered in 1864 while returning from Arizona with a large amount of gold.

At Mason Valley, about 8 miles beyond Vallecito, it turned off from the main trail, heading toward the eastern slope of the Cuyamacas, following the same route pioneered by Pedro Fages some seventy years earlier, through Oriflamme Canon to a small plateau near the top. It then crossed over the rim into Cuyamaca Valley and headed south to Green Valley and site of Lasitor's mountain home.

It was about 7 miles from Lassitor's down Green Valley to Guatay Valley and "Julian's" place (Sandoval's); another 7 more miles to William's in Valle de las Viejas, then 14 miles to Ames's at Los Coches, 16 more to Mission San Diego, and a final 5 miles to the western terminal of the San Antonio & San Diego Mail Line at the Plaza in Old San Diego.

Birch's route and mode of transportation was similar to that used from 1853 to 1856 when San Warnock and Joe Swycaffer packed the US Army mail on mules semi-weekly from Fort Yuma to San Diego. Both Warnock and Swycaffer later played key roles as early settlers in Julian and Ballena.

Some writers erroneously refer to the Warnock/Swycaffer Army mail service as the "Jack-Ass Mail", but the term was not coined until after those two had been discharged from the Army and were farmers.

The "Jack-Ass Mail" lasted but three years. James E. Birch, its founder, was lost at sea in the sinking of a steamer, just four days after his first mail run reached San Diego in September 1857. The company passed through several ownerships but never made money. The Post Office Department cancelled its contracts.

The Butterfield System lasted but a year longer, until the Civil War shut down private mail service to the west.

Cuyamaca trails saw little white man traffic during the war years and up until 1870. But once gold was discovered, the trail through Green Valley to Guatay, Viejas and on to San Diego was well used by wagons bringing in supplys and shipping out precious metal.

THE PONY EXPRESS

The first regular mail service to Julian was carried by a young enterprising man destined later to play a big role in San Diego County affairs. Chester Gunn, while in his early 20s established a pony express mail service between San Diego and Julian in 1871.

It was just hard work, with little romance. Julian had

CHESTER GUNN
operated the first regular
mail service to Julian,
riding pony express over
the Indian trails from San
Diego to the mines. He
was also one of the first
apple growers in the area.
Gunn went on to become a
San Diego County Supervisor.

grown overnight and was only reached by long, rough roads over which supplies were hauled by wagon. Mail service was catch-as-catch-can, and received only when some trustworthy person was going that way. There were no stage lines yet and no way to reach the back country except to buy or hire a rig to make the two-day journey.

In a 1924 interview with the San Diego Union, Mr. Gunn recalled, *"It seemed to me that there ought to be good money in fast service. I was out of a job just then, so I started this pony express on my own responsibility. I charged ten cents a letter and carried letters and small packages. The people up there were glad to pay that much for they knew they'd get their mail as soon as it came in, instead of having to wait until someone happened to be going up.*

"In those days San Diego got its mail by ship. A ship came in once a week. For a long time it had only been once a month, but as the town grew, it was increased to a ship every two weeks, and later to a week. I only made one trip a week to Julian, but I made the trip in good time and regularly, and the people depended on me." Instead of traveling the long, slow wagon road, which was about 80 miles long, Gunn was able to make the trip up in one day by following the Indian trails up into the Cajon Valley, then the length of the San Vicente Rancho to Ballena, through Santa Ysabel to Julian. As we drive today along Wildcat Canyon Road through the Barona and San Vicente Valleys on to Vista Ramona Road and the Old Julian Road we get some idea of the terrain through which Gunn made his way.

"It was a hard trip. I started the service in the fall and kept it up all through the winter, about six months. I had to make the trip in all kinds of weather, wet and sloppy, muddy, slippery trails, and cold winds with sleet and snow."

But as soon as stages started making the trip in one day, Gunn added, *"there was no use for my pony express."*

Gunn went on to become Julian's Wells Fargo agent in 1870, and later, the first postmaster of the town's new post office. He tried his hand at mining and is said to have planted some of the first apple trees in the area. In 1889, Governor Waterman appointed him to an unexpired term on the County Board of Supervisors and he was later elected, in his own right, to one term.

Chester Gunn later served on the commission that split off parts of San Diego County to create the new counties of Riverside in 1893 and Imperial in 1907.

THE STAGE

In the spring of 1870, North and Knight began operating a twice-weekly stage to Julian City through Santa Ysabel and Santa Maria Valley. But they were soon run out of business during a slow period in 1870 by William Tweed.

Tweed's coaches left San Diego on Mondays and Thursdays at 6 a.m. and returned on Tuesdays and Fridays. Stewart and Reed's office on 6th near J Street, or Tweed's house on E Street near 1st served as the stage stations. The fare to Julian was $6, but the return trip was $4.

Tweed managed to command all the stage business until the summer of 1872 when Adolph Stokes and son Edward secured a mail contract and started a second stage line to the mines. The Stokeses were son and grandson of Captain Edward Stokes, grantee to Ranchos Santa Maria and Santa Ysabel. Their home, which still stands today and is beautifully restored, is situated on Highway 78 just east of Magnolia Road in Ramona.

The fierce competition that soon developed became ledgendary. James Jasper wrote about it in his memoirs in 1928. *"Seems that Adolph Stokes, who owned the Santa Maria Rancho, was well stocked with horses. Seeing an opportunity for some profitable employment he decided to go into competition with the Tweed Stage line, and a spirited rivalry followed. Fares were cut and re-cut, foreshadowing the survival of the fittest, until passengers could ride the 60 miles between San Diego and Julian free. Then the opposition line offered one dollar to each passenger that rode with their driver. That seemed the limit, but it was not, for the next day the old line offered passengers one dollar each and free drinks on the way. The free drinks won and the opposition went out of business."*

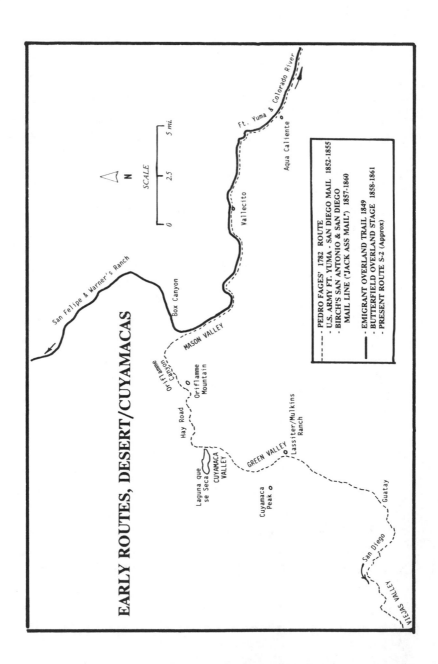

EARLY ROUTES, DESERT/CUYAMACAS

N

SCALE

0   2.5   5 mi.

------- PEDRO FAGES' 1782 ROUTE
— · — · U.S. ARMY FT. YUMA - SAN DIEGO MAIL 1852-1855
— — BIRCH'S SAN ANTONIO & SAN DIEGO
MAIL LINE ('JACK ASS MAIL') 1857-1860
· · · · · EMIGRANT OVERLAND TRAIL 1849
— · · — BUTTERFIELD OVERLAND STAGE 1858-1861
————— PRESENT ROUTE S-2 (Approx)

Ft. Yuma & Colorado River

Aqua Caliente

Vallecito

San Felipe & Warner's Ranch

Box Canyon

MASON VALLEY

Oriflamme Canyon

Oriflamme Mountain

Hay Road

Laguna que se Seca

CUYAMACA VALLEY

Cuyamaca Peak

Lassiter/Mulkins Ranch

GREEN VALLEY

Guatay

San Diego

VIEJAS VALLEY

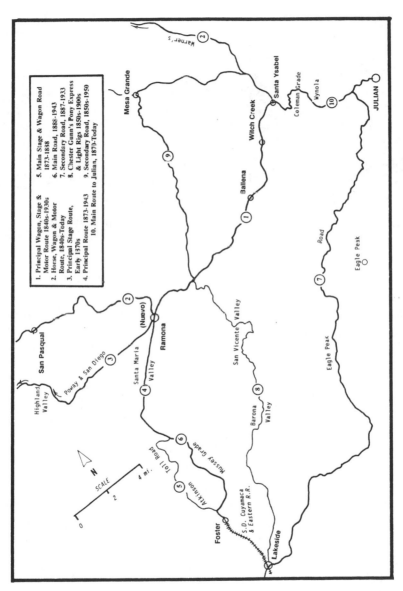

EARLY ROUTES, JULIAN/SAN DIEGO

A dispatch appearing in the July 28, 1872 edition of the San Diego Daily World described how competition extended beyond fares. In it we get a first-hand account of a frantic race down the grades between these two competitors, Tweed's Pioneer Line and Stokes' Mail Stage, written by a passenger who was a Julian businessman and also served as stringer for the World. "EXCITING RACE BETWEEN THE PIONEER AND MAIL STAGE FROM JULIAN - TWO HORSES RUINED"

From Col. Hopkins, of Julian City, and others we learn the following: At 6:20 A.M. of yesterday, "George" cried "all aboard" and almost instanter six passengers were rapidly whirled out of Julian, in one of Tweed's pioneer stages, drawn by four swift horses. Before reaching Rock Springs, the rumbling Stokes' mail stage was heard, and a look back revealed, amid clouds of dust, the dim outline of four horses on the full run. Soon the "Mail Stage", with two or three passengers, and Stokes himself for driver, came thundering alongside of the "Pioneer" and made a spendid effrt to "pass". All was now excitment, drivers, horses and passengers, all anxious to run, except the Col. who is religiously oppossed to racing. The wheels whizzed, the horses' feet clattering, drivers cracked their whips and lashed their panting, foaming coursers, clouds of dust filled the air and the excited passengers joined in the general din and "made the confusion worst confounded." Now the Pioneer would shoot ahead, and anon the Mail would lap and make a desparate but vain effort to lead George. This exciting and hazardous racing was kept up till near Rock Springs, when one of Stokes' horses stepped in a squirrel hole and broke his leg. The animal was quickly stripped of his harness, and the Mail went, drawn by three horses. While the Pioneer was hastly dining and changing horses, Stokes got ahead. Soon one of his overheated horses "gave

F.R. SAWDAY'S GENERAL STORE was located at Witch Creek and served settlers of Ballena as well as Julian. It was an important stop for the stages that operated between San Diego and the back country. The main store building shown in this 1886 photo still survives as part of the descendants' home buildings, painted dark green today and located on the south side of the road going to Santa Ysabel.

out" and falling down, was stripped and rolled into a gulch. At Babb's, Stokes got fresh horses, and driving furiously kept the lead, and arrived in the city several miles in advance of the Pioneer. George, supposing that the Mail had taken the usual "Mail" route via Old Town, and some miles out of the way, and supposing also that the Pioneer was ahead, came in more leisurely - and behind.

Racing is always interesting because exciting, yet, we hope, bothe lines have shown their "metal" and "bottom", will, for the sake of the traveling public and poor horses, go at a moderate pace, except when the World is aboard. *

Rock Springs was located just north of present

---

* This news account also appeared in the author's book "Ramona and Round About".

intersection of Poway and Pomerado Roads, and Babb's later became known as Big Springs Lodge and Poway Grove.

So much for the laissez-faire frontier transportation system.

ATKINSON TOLL ROAD

By 1873, if not long before, it had become clear to all that a more direct route to Julian had to be developed. In that year, two enterprising brothers, Lemuel and Henry Atkinson saw an opportunity to cash in on the bad road system. The two had earlier moved from Sacramento to work at the Golden Chariot where Lemuel was mine foreman.

They studied the various possible routes and filed on land at the north end of what is now Mussey Grade Road in Ramona. In 1873 they built their Atkinson toll road to the west of the present Mussey alignment. After operating and maintaining it for a year, however, they apparently figured they could make more money selling it to the County, and they did, for $1,700. Henry Atkinson was appointed roadmaster for the district by the board of supervisors.

The Atkinson Road proved a real tough one to maintain. It was very steep in places, and when heavy rains came, it was a nightmare for teamsters to negotiate.

And heavy rains did come. The winter of 1873-74 was esecially hard on shipping in and out of Julian. In December it began to rain heavily and continued into the new year. Snow and 15 inches of rain in the San Felipe Canyon shut down the Golden Chariot. Work on one mine after another came to a halt. Rains washed out the roads and wagons were unable to move ore to the stamp mills. Telegraph lines were down. Cattle sank up to their bellies in mud.

By February, when the ground became soaked to a depth of three feet, all transportation between San Diego and the mines came to a standstill. And then that was followed by another 15 inches of rain and snow. Not until the end of March were freight wagons able to haul their cargo to the mountains.

But the Atkinson toll road was a main stage and freight link to Julian and the back country and had to be relied upon for several years to come.

On April 25, 1883, the San Diego Union reported, "the road from the head of Atkinson grade to the Cajon is a disgrace to the County - it could hardly be in worse condition." Three weeks later Joseph Foster was appointed overseer for that road district. But in spite of working long hard hours, Foster couldn't keep up with it.

THE MUSSEY GRADE ROAD

A more managable alignment was needed and in October 1883 the impatient settlers in the back country presented the board of supervisors with a petition to replace the Atkinson. A survey had determined that a route through Mussey's Canyon to the east would result in a much more favorable grade. While the Atkinson grade ran 30"-33" to the rod or 15 to 17 percent in many areas, the Mussey route could be built to an average road grade of 9 inches to the rod, or 4.5 percent.

Despite private subscriptions from citizens in Julian, Santa Maria Valley and Ballena to help finance construction, it wasn't until December 1886 that the county was able to finish the road.

The Mussey Grade Road proved to be the main link between San Diego and Julian for 50 years. Construction

FOSTER'S STATION was the end of the line for the San Diego Cuyamaca and Eastern Railroad. From here the traveller to the mountains boarded a Concord stage coach. The route took them up the old Mussey Grade to Ramona, Ballena, Santa Ysabel and on to either Julian or the 'springs' at Warner's. This picture was taken about 1910, just before Joe Foster phased out horsepower in favor of motor stages. Note the early motorcycle.

of the San Vicente dam in the early 1940s blocked its right of way and this route was replaced in 1943 by State Highway 67.

THE RAIL LINK TO JULIAN

The San Diego, Cuyamaca and Eastern Railroad was built in 1888-89 and ran from San Diego to Foster, just north of Lakeside. Its principal organizer was former California Governor Robert W. Waterman, and owner of the Stonewall Mine in Cuyamaca.

The line started at the foot of N Street in San Diego and ran 23 miles through Lemon Grove, La Mesa and

MOTOR STAGES replaced the horse-drawn variety in 1911. Shown here, about 1913 in front of the Kennelworth Inn in Ramona, are the two Mack Truck 12 passenger mail stages Joe Foster operated between Julian and the San Diego Cuyamaca and Eastern RR station at Foster.

Lakeside, terminating at Fosters, just south of the present San Vicente dam. He and his investors envisioned a railroad that would go all the way up the grade to Julian and to his Cuyamaca mine. It was said that this railroad, under construction in 1888, *"will undoubtedly infuse new energy into these districts, and induce capital to develop the many promising ledges that have been partially opened."* But the promoters ran out of capital before they could get it into the mountains.

San Diego newspapers were replete with reports between 1892 and 1909 telling of the efforts, trials and tribulations of back country leaders to get the railroad extended up the mountain to their towns. A railroad would bring growth and success to any aspiring young town like Ramona and Ballena. Many a family fortune was invested in new townsite land that might someday become more valuable when the railroad finally reached them. But it was not to be.

The San Diego, Cuyamaca and Eastern Railroad never earned the money its investors expected. Capital requiremnets and operating costs would not allow further expansion, and back country guaranteees of revenue did not materialize.

But the S.D.C.&E. RR did provide a vital transportation link to Julian. Joseph Foster owned the ranch where the tracks terminated. He also, along with partner A.P. Frary ran the main stage line into Julian and Warners, via Ramona, Ballena and Santa Ysabel. Passengers and freight made the transfer from rail car to stage coach at Foster's and proceeded to their mountain destinations.

By 1916, the S.D.C.& E. RR was out of business. The great flood of 1916 washed out much of the railroad's track. With the advent of motorcars, and improvements to the road system, there was no finacial incentive to rebuild.

THE BANNER GRADE

Discovery of gold in Banner, six miles east of Julian, created a major transportion problem. Julian and Banner were always well linked socially and commercially, but from a road standpoint, the link was very weak one indeed. It was well nigh impossible to get machinery in to work those mines at the bottom of the hill. The grade was so steep that machinery was loaded on "stone sleds" and lowered by ropes one thousand feet down the mountain via what was known as "the slide". Wagons had

BANNER GRADE ROAD TODAY is no freeway by current standards, but a vast improvement over the Wilcox Toll Road of the nineteenth century. Banner is seen in this aerial shot in the lower left corner and Julian at the top.

THE COLEMAN TOLL STATION about 1895. The Coleman grade road came up to Wynola from Santa Ysabel.

to have poles run between their spokes and a tree dragged behind in order to keep them from running up on the heels of the mules pulling them.

A wagon road with tolerable grade had been surveyed to the mines in San Felipe Canyon by October 1870, but was not completed until the middle of 1871. This was a six to seven mile toll road around "Gold Hill" and down the wooded canyon. It was operated by Horace Wilcox who extracted twenty-five cents for a cart, buggy or wagon with one horse or mule. The rate went up to fifty cents for a two horse rig and a dollar for a loaded four horse wagon. Twelve and a half cents was charged for a saddle horse, loose stock three cents per head, and so on.

8

Fact 'n Fiction

Most towns have an historical legend or two. Julian is no exception. One such has persisted for nearly a century, and is still being told with great enthusiasm today. It is the claim that in 1872 or '73 or '74 or '75, (the year depends on who tells the story), Julian rivaled the City of San Diego for location of the San Diego County seat.

There is no reference to such an election in the newspapers or official records during that period. But the story keeps popping up none the less in travel guides, newspaper and magazine feature articles. Even some noted historians in San Diego have aided and abetted in perpetuating the tale by quoting old timers who spoke about it - - but not expanding on the subject nor verifying or debunking it either.

It seems the tale established a firm foothold in twentieth century newsprint stemming primarily from accounts told by at least four Julian pioneers. One was

Mrs. L.S. Wellington, a daughter of Drue Bailey. Other sources were Miss Maud L. Kelly, Margaret Grand Farmer, and of course Julian's premier story teller James Jasper, who had his version as well.

The Kelly interview was conducted in 1939 by Winifred Davidson, active member of the San Diego Historical Society: *"The meeting where a vote was taken as to whether San Diego or Julian was to be the county seat was held at the Paine home in San Pascual,"* Maud Kelly recalled, *"Walter Paine was a little boy and he remembers about it. He says the San Diego delegates got one of the Julian delegates intoxicated and the result was a vote in favor of San Diego."*

The Wellington interview appeared in the December 31, 1939 edition of the San Diego Union. *"As for the battle to change the county seat, Mrs Wellington recalls that her father used to relate how he and his townsmen promised not to bring up the issue again provided there might always be a Julian man in the courthouse."*

Margaret Grand Farmer's version was related as recently as 1973 in an interview with a local history student. She said she was convinced such an event occurred, stating she first heard of it soon after moving to Julian in 1909.

One example of how far a reporter's imagination will go to add color to a feature story, is quoted from the San Diego Evening Tribune, March 14, 1959 edition:

"Sinfulness was costly in 1872 with a population of more than 3,000, Julian challenged San Diego for the county seat. Julian lost the election by three votes. San Diego politicians came to the mining town and kept the saloons full, setting up drinks for miners who should have been voting."

James Jasper, consummate Julian supporter, newspaper man and County Supervisor gave his version in an

JULIAN CITY ABOUT 1873 Earliest known photo of the town. Population was estimated at less than 400. The City of San Diego had about 5,000 then. Stories have persisted over the years, however, that Julian came within a few votes of winning an election to move the County seat there from San Diego.

unpublished manuscript written in 1928. Jasper liked to tell a good story, polishing and embellishing as he went along. How much of his version is fact or fiction is not known.

But according to Jasper, the situation developed *"in 1875, when Julian had grown to imposing stature and occupied second place of importance in the county, and demanded certain recognition at the hands of the powers that be at the County Seat. Failing to impress the county officials with their importance, they rebelled and threatened to call an election and move the County Seat to Julian, and at that time they had the votes to carry out the threat."* Jasper continues, *"That fact made the politicians set up and take notice; they put their think tanks to working, and decided to hold both the Democratic and Republican conventions in Julian in an effort to head off the move. As a further harmony move, the Republicans nominated Julian's adopted son, Joseph Coyne, for County Sheriff, and the Democrats gave Julian the Supervisor."*

The August 6, 1873 edition of the San Diego Union confirms that the County Democratic Party Convention was indeed held in Julian. County elections that year were quite spirited. According to newspaper accounts, rallies for both the Democratic and Republican candidates were held in Julian that year.

It would seem then, that the event that most likely provided the basis for these stories stemmed from a political contest, all right, and it was fought in 1873 between Julian and San Diego City, sure enough. But it was not over the site of the County seat. It was over the location of the Democrat's convention that year.

In 1873 San Diego had a population that was estimated by the San Diego Union Weekly at 4,960. While it has been commonly said that Julian's population during the boom years of the early 70s was as large as San Diego's, the records don't substantiate anything more than 600 residents in and about Julian at any time in the early '70s. The 1870 census which was taken at the height of the gold rush showed 574 total. Julian was recognized as a township for that particular census. Soon after that, however, an exodus of sorts took place due to the attempted Cuyamaca boundary float. Also, gold was discovered in Banner in the fall of 1870, and many of the Julian miners and families shifted their interests and residences there. By the time 1880 rolled around, the census takers called the area "Aqua Caliente Township" which took in territory including Banner and Cuyamaca. The total count for the township in June 1880 was 499.

But while the larger City of San Diego was predominately Republican, stemming from its Union ties during the Civil war, Julian politics was dominated by Confederate veterans who were strongly Democrat and exerted themselves accordingly. So when it came time for the Democratic convention in 1873, Julian made a move to host it.

The matter apparently was settled in the Paine home in San Pascual by a vote of county Democratic leaders. What Walter Paine later remembered overhearing when he was a small boy was indeed a matter of some political import at the time. But it didn't involve moving the county seat, just the seat of San Diego County's Democratic political power for an election year convention.

THE STAGE COACH ROBBERY

What good is a history book about gold mining country without at least one tale of a stage coach robbery. So here it is, from the San Diego Union, February 25, 1875.

The gold that was produced in Julian had to be transported out, and much of it was carried by the Wells, Fargo & Co. stages. About dusk on a Monday evening late in February, 1875, two highwaymen stopped the stage seven miles out of Julian City while it was slowly climbing a steep grade. The robbers demanded the treasure box, which contained $1,000. The driver refused, telling them if they wanted it they would have to come get it. While one bandit covered the driver with a double-barreled shotgun, the other climbed up and handed down the box.

The highwayman broke it open and took out only the money. There had been four passengers aboard the stage, but at the foot of the grade three had got out to walk on ahead. The fourth, an invalid, remained in the stage. After the money box was thrown down, the robbers orded the driver to go on. They broke open the box, grabbed the money, and disappeared. When the driver reported the hold-up in Julian, a posse tried to pick up the tracks of the robbers, but in vain. Wells, Fargo immediately offered a handsome reward of $750 for the arrest of these two gunmen, but nothing was ever heard of them afterward.

A story concerning the outcome of this event circulated for a period of time, however, but wasn't related in print until some 60 years later, in the Union edition of October 1, 1936.

Seems it centered on a gaudily dressed man who was often seen in Julian City about that time. He was a gambler known as "Slim Jim", who wore a high hat and frock coat, and who disliked work but had a fondness for flashy jewelry.

Slim made friends with a Wells Fargo express driver by the name of Hicks who took the stage to Santa Ysabel. Soon after the hold-up by the two masked men, Hicks was fired by Wells Fargo.

Though he was out of work, Hicks bought a horse and buggy and along with his friend Slim, visited Banner every day for a month. The two men of leisure exhibited their prosperity liberally in saloons and amusement parlors in both Julian and Banner. But no one was ever able to prove a thing.

9
Town Neighbors

When L.B. Redman stumbled unto a rich gold bearing quartz ledge while gathering wild berries in San Felipe Canyon, Julian City was less than a year old.

This was in September 1870, and the chunk of gold bearing quartz Redman brought back to town set off a new rush. Suddenly the hills and canyons to the east of Julian were swarming with prospectors. Ore veins twelve to fifteen inches wide were reported.

Redman marked his claim by setting a small American flag atop a pile of rocks. The town of Banner, which soon developed in the nearby canyon, took its name from Redman's flag.

More rich discoveries followed. The Baileys' Ready Relief, the Montezuma, Madden, King Williams, City of Paris and the Gebhardt indicated there was a definite mineral belt extending from the Van Wert to the Redman.

The first gold quartz was crushed in mortars and the gold panned from gravel and sand. Next, arestras were set up in the canyon and operated by either mules or humans. By mid-October there were twelve to fourteen arestras running and the San Diego Union reported that even a mill had been set up by a Mr. Hamlet, late of Julian. The correspondent hastened to clarify that the mill was not for crushing ore, but for making whiskey.

By November 27 there were eighty to ninety miners busy in the canyon and they decided it was time to form their own mining district. The San Filipe Rancho grant formed its eastern boundary and the Cuyamaca its western, so the new district was "free from the cloud of (Mexican) grants", so reported the Union. Michael S.Julian was elected recorder of the Banner Mining District.

During 1871 Banner was growing by leaps and bounds - mainly at the expense of Julian City. Not only were the diggin's rich, but a miner in San Felipe Canyon didn't have to worry about those Cuyamaca rapscallions trying to steal his claim. New "diggins" were multiplying rapidly.

With all this activity, a town site called Banner City was laid out on about the only level land in the canyon. A wagon road from Julian was surveyed and was completed with an acceptable grade. This was a six to seven mile route around "Gold Hill" and down the heavily wooded canyon operated by Horace Wilcox.

Prior to the construction of this road, the route was so difficult that a slide was used down the steep mountain. Mining equipment, machinery, and provisions were lashed to a sled which was lowered by ropes over 1,000 feet down the steep slopes. A tree was tied behind the sled to serve as a brake.

BANNER CITY

Banner City in the summer of 1872 consisted of several stores, a boarding house, two quartz mills and several residences surrounded by the desolate, chaparral covered mountains.

By 1874 there was no doubt Banner was for real. In July a San Diego Union reporter glowingly wrote:

"Two months ago only a few cabins claimed the attention of the resident, or visitor. Now forty buildings, mills, business houses, and dwellings are nestled together in this beautiful little mountain valley, united, claim themselves to be now and in time to come the Banner City of all the mining districts of California..."

After 1874, both Julian and Banner declined. Free milling gold became scarce, and the other mines were too expensive to work. The big strike in Tombestone, Arizona lured many miners away, and others turned to farming and raising stock.

The Julian and Banner Mining districts consolidated in 1881. With discovery of the Gold King and Gold Queen activity in the two areas picked up again. But through the years the fortunes of Banner would boom and fade and boom again.

By 1892, twenty years after the little town got its start, it was again a thriving back country community. Mining had made it what it was, and when capital from outside the state was in evidence, the town was healthy.

The stream that flowed through the town was normally a gentle, rippling stream. But during a prolonged heavy storm it was capable of washing out half the town. Such a storm happened during the winter of 1873-74. However the town folk rebuilt and went on as before. Storms in 1916 and 1926 again raised havoc with the town. After 1926 little was left to remind the visitor of Banner's once proud presence.

Today all that remains is a general store with gas pump to service the busy traveler on his trips to and from the desert.

OTHER TOWNS & DREAMS

Banner City wasn't the only potential town to rival Julian City. During the gold mining days at least four other budding villages made a bid for a spot on the San Diego County map. They were Eastwood, Branson City, Cuyamaca City and Lick Skillet.

BRANSON CITY

Soon after the discovery of gold in Julian, Lewis C. Branson, a San Diego lawyer decided to lay out another town site. It was about one mile east of Drury Bailey's and was named Branson City. It contained 96 lots, many of which were named for U.S. Presidents.

Branson built a store, saloon, boarding house and dance hall. But his new town didn't grow and develop as expected. In fact it was a flop.

The entire town, which was located in the general vicinity of Julian's present day high school was sold for $20 to H.D. Reynolds on April 3, 1872.

EASTWOOD

Even Julian City's first merchant, the enterprising Joe Swycaffer decided to take a run at new town development. He plotted a town one mile west of Julian, on part of Chester Gunn's ranch and placed the lots on the market. Swycaffer named it Eastwood. What it was 'east of' we don't know. But it didn't develop either.

Much of the reason these two towns didn't sell had to do with the fact the promoters couldn't deliver clear title to any lots they sold. This was a period when land rights in the area were in a turmoil with the ongoing dispute between the owners of the Cuyamaca Rancho and the settlers of Julian City. Until that issue was settled in late 1873, nobody in the area knew for sure if the land he settled on was "Government Land", which could be legally homesteaded, or if it would be taken away from him as part of the Mexican Grant land grab.

In promoting Julian City, Drue Bailey recognized this dilemma. He essentially gave his city lots away to anyone who would build a home on them. By the time the boundary dispute was finally settled, there was enough in the way of improvements to keep the town alive and growing. Then he was able to get the $50 to $100 a lot being asked.

LICK SKILLET

And yes - there was even talk of starting a new town called "Lick Skillet" near Banner. While official records contain no reference to such a development, a small item in the June 6, 1890 edition of the Julian Sentinel told of plans for such.

"L.L. Wilcox will soon lay out a town site on the ground once known as "Lick Skillet". That name originated as follows: When the mines were first struck at Banner, they panned out so rich that the boys could find no one who was willing to do the cooking, so they had to take turns about licking the skillet".

We don't know if Wilcox was really serious about such a town, or if this was just one of the knee-slappers going around Julian at the time. We know the Wilcox boys liked a good laugh and editor Jasper also liked to spice up his paper with humor. You be the judge.

CUYAMACA CITY

Cuyamaca City was a different development altogether. It was a company town built and operated by the man who eventually bought the Stonewall Mine and developed it to its most successful level of operation. Governor Robert Waterman purchased the mine along with approximately 26,000 acres of the Cuyamaca Rancho in 1886. The town that soon developed was located just north of the mine on Lake Cuyamaca.

At its height of activity, the Stonewall mine employed 250 workers. They and their families had to be housed and Waterman built a town to accommodate them.

There was a two story hotel "with bath rooms", a bunkhouse to accommodate sixty, cottages for the married miners, a general store, barn, corral, a schoolhouse and postoffice.

Cuyamaca City offered its residents many progressive amenities. Water was run through one-inch pipes from a main reservoir to each of the cottages, bunk houses, hotel and mine buildings. The town was connected with the City of San Diego by one of the first long distance telephone lines in 1894. It had its own full-time physician. The town had the distinction of having one of the first public libraries in the region, and while it's not known how many volumes it contained, it created quite a stir in neighboring Julian. The editor of the Julian Sentinel challenged his readers in the November 21, 1890 edition: *"Why can't we have a public library in Julian when the Stonewall has one?"*

But the town never-the-less was a company town. and the Watermans kept a tight rein on it. The miners didn't own their homes, and further more, no liquor was allowed. If the boys wanted to drink they just had to go to Julian City.

STONEWALL MINE was by far the best gold producer of all the mines in the area. It accounted for a total of $2 million out of an estimated grand total for all mines in the Julian, Banner and Cuyamaca region of $5 million. During the late 1880s it employed about 250 men. Originally named in honor of Confederates' hero General Stonewall Jackson, the Jackson part was quickly dropped when the original owners realized the name offended potential investors with strong Union loyalties.

With Governor Waterman's death in 1891, and resulting financial problems, the mine operation was cutback and the town went into decline.

Toward the end of the 1890s and a for a few years into the early 20th century, the hotel was operated as a resort catering to duck hunters and fishermen. But by 1905, the once prosperous town's population had declined to but 50 residents from a peak of about 500 just fifteen years earlier and in 1907 the San Diego County Directory listed but 11 residents.

CUYAMACA CITY was a company town sited on the south shore of Lake Cuyamaca and built by Stonewall Mine owner Governor Waterman. It boasted this two story hotel as well as cottages for the married workers, bunkhouses for sixty men, a general store, schoolhouse and postoffice. At its peak in the late 1880s, it had a population of nearly 500. After mining operations were cut back, the hotel was operated for several years around the turn of the century as a resort catering to fishermen and duck hunters.

Cuyamaca City and the Stonewall Mine were dismantled in 1923 by the new owner of the Rancho, Ralph Dyer. He sold the dilapidated buildings to anyone interested in moving them, and the mine machinery for scrap metal.

Unless one is familiar with the history of the area, the average park visitor would be hard pressed to know there was once a thriving town on the south shore of Lake Cuyamaca. However if he strolls up the knoll above the fenced mine shaft opening, he might find a covered brick hexagon reservoir. This is the same reservoir the Watermans built to supply water to their old company town.

10
Editor and the Law

Julian has had several newspapers and periodicals during its 120 years of life. But the town didn't have its first until nearly 17 years after it was born. The *JULIAN SENTINEL,* while not actually conceived by James Jasper, was brought into this world by him gasping and coughing in 1887.

Jasper wrote two histories of Julian, neither of which was published. *JULIAN and ROUNDABOUT* was written in 1928. Its double spaced manuscript ran 68 pages.

Six years later he had produced a much more detailed work running nearly 400 pages and covering more back country territory. Titled *TRAIL-BREAKERS AND HISTORY MAKERS,* the sub-title told its scope, *"of Julian - Ballena - Mesa Grande - Oak Grove - Warner Ranch - Banner - Cuyamaca in San Diego County California, History - Biography - Reminiscences".* He attempted to raise subscriptions for its publication. This was during the heart of the great depression, however, and capital was in short supply. But lack of money wasn't the book's only obstacle. Jasper included several character profiles among the biographies which some surviving family members considered less than flattering. It is said he was threatened with legal action should the work be published.

JULIAN'S FIRST NEWSPAPER

Jasper told how Julian got its first newspaper and how he in turn broke into the business in his 1928 manuscript, to wit:

"The dawn of 1887 found the people of Julian rioting in new-born courage and ripe for exploitation. New settlers were coming in and building new homes. Orchards, vineyards and gardens were again being planted, new schools were being established, countless cattle roamed the hills, the mining industry had taken on a new lease of life, old shafts were being re-opened, miners were delving into the earth and bringing up golden treasurer, and once again stamps were dropping on pay ore.

"Such were the flattering prospects of camp just seventeen years after the discovery of the Washington Mine, which lured A.J. Jenkins to camp. He came unheralded, dropped off with a printer's rule and shooting stick and the startling information that Julian was in sore need of a newspaper, and that he had come with the brains and experience to start it, provided the people would finance the enterprise in the sum of $600. Of course the $600 was a gift, a subsidy for the public benefit.

"A meeting was called, the bait swallowed, hook, line and sinker, the money raised, the plant installed, and on March 14, 1887 the first issue of The Julian Sentinel appeared as a six-column quarto with patent innards and boiler-plate veneer. The writer put $20 in the pot and drew a bunch of trouble, as will soon appear.

VENERABLE JAMES JASPER posing in later years as the Julian Constable he once was.

"The Sentinel plant was parked in the lean-to of Hale & Porter's saloon, the only available place in town; the room had but one door, and it opened out onto the main street. On a Sunday evening, shortly after the paper was established, Sam Porter, in cold blood, shot and killed an unarmed Mexican in front of the Sentinel office, and his lifeless body crumpled down in the door where it remained until the justice of the peace (acting coroner) arrived, held an inquest and removed the corpse. Porter put out a plea of self defense, and as there was no effort made to get conflicting evidence, he was exonerated. It was over in

thirty minutes.

"All that time I lived three miles out of town, but such news travels fast, and I soon heard of the murder. The Saturday following I went to town, got the Sentinel and scanned its columns, even to the patent, for the account of the murder, but no mention of it could I find. I had never been inside a printing office, but I was hot, and with the Sentinel still in hand I walked in and asked Jenkins who did his reporting. "I do it myself," he replied. "Why do you ask?"

"I heard there was a murder in town Sunday, but no one would ever know it by reading the Sentinel," I answered, "Why don't you hire a small boy, perhaps he wouldn't overlook a little thing like murder." "Where were you when this killing was done?"

"Me!" he exclaimed. "I was right here in the office and couldn't get out; the man fell right in the office door; don't you see the blood there? It would have been as much of my life is worth to have mentioned the matter, for Hale came in here next morning and told me if I mentioned the killing he would blow up the office and me with it.

"So that's the way the wind blows is it?" I said. "Well Jenkins, I'll say you are not the man to run a paper in a mining camp like Julian."

"Don't I know it now," he replied. "If I could only get away I would go today."

"Well," said I, "how much cash will it take to get you on your way?"

"Six hundred dollars and I'll be glad to go." he answered.

*"Well" said I, "put that in writing, give me a week's time and if I can find a man in the mountains who can get out a paper, you can go." When I left the office I carried an option on the plant."**

As it developed, Jasper was unable to find anyone in

---

* This account also appeared in the author's book "Ramona and Round About".

the area interested in taking over the paper. He did find a local school teacher, W.A. Sickler, who agreed to take over the editing and management, but only if Jasper rode herd on the finances.

Jasper was very much a 'hands on' publisher with the paper's editorial content reflecting his combative, jabbing and oft times fun loving personality. He reported the bad with the good, and tried to provide the town with a conscience. In June 1893, he moved the paper to Nuevo (later renamed Ramona) where population growth appeared to be more favorable than Julian's, and where the Sentinel continues to be published today, some 100 years later.

Jasper served on the San Diego County Board of Supervisors from 1893 until 1905 and sold the Sentinel in 1894 in order to devote more time to his supervisorial duties. He was later quoted as saying, *"I ran that newspaper nine years, and then gave it away and made a better bargain than when I bought it. Never in the time I owned it did it pay expenses for a single month."*

The following was reprinted from an 1890 edition of the Julian Sentinel. The yellowed clipping was saved by Horace Wilcox and given to Timothy Brownhill in 1914 for publication in a special edition of the Ramona Sentinel. It gives the reader a view of the mining camp through the jesting eyes of Jasper. He enjoyed poking fun, even at himself, and in those days not much concern was openly expressed over that which we refer to today as "ethnic or racial insensitivity", by either the giver, or receiver of the jabs.

"ED. SENTINEL:- A gentleman from San Diego, while at the Hot Springs, happened to meet one of our Julian small boys; and having some curiosity to know something of the town, enquired of him concerning the people and business, and he gave him the following birds-eye view".

"Well, the first place you come to is the post office. Horace Wilcox, he keeps that. He is the best story teller in town, but he has to use his hands and feet in tellin' a story. He can't tell any now for he has a sore foot. The doctor says he cut one of the 'tendons' that connects his tongue with his foot. He gets cranky, too, when we make a noise while he calls the mail.

"The next place is Tom Daly's butcher shop. He's made many a "stack" and is now able to build himself a nice, new shop. He's cranky, too.

"Then comes Jasper & Sickler. They got the newspaper and sell real estate. The little fellow is Jim Jasper. He tells all the lies about the country and the other fellow prints them. Jenkins the printer, is with them and so is Bob Marlette - he's the devil.

"Then comes Charley Hale's saloon. That's a kind of Mexican outfit. Plenty to eat though. Then Jo Marks, the Jew, keeps the big brick store. My pa hauls freight for him. He's mighty close, though.

"Then there's the saloon on the corner. You might think he's a Mexican, but he ain't, that's Jeff Williams.

"Across the street is the Mountain View Hotel. Garland thinks he runs that, but he don't; its his wife.

"Across the street in another saloon you'll find a long-legged fellow. That's Bill Decker. He'll ask you in to have a drink and a bully good time. Frank Stanford is there, but you must be easy with him or he'll get mad.

"Then comes Wellington's carpenter shop. He and Geo. Johnson is always busy doing nothing.

"Fred Acker got married on the strength of the Lone Oak, but when that fizzled his daddy in law fired him.

"Bally and my pa haul freight from San Diego and they blow a great deal about their big loads (of beer.)

"Around the corner is Joe, the blacksmith. He's busy from five o'clock in the morning drinking beer and pounding iron.

"The next is Ben Simmons. He's got two or three Injin ponies and thinks he keeps a livery stable. He charges first class prices and is hunting some one to shake dice for ten cents, if he wins. He don't beat, he jumps the game. Come over some time and see Lee Williams and his cane. He's a dude."

Yes, Jasper liked to poke fun, and he was always trying to stir things up. But mostly, he was Julian City's champion. And every now and then he would try to start a feud with the big city fellows from the San Diego daily papers about how Julian was better, or they were worse, or whatever, and when they took the bait, the verbal barbs would fly. This was his way of having fun with a newspaper. Might as well, he wasn't making any money at it.

JULIAN'S TOWN HALLS

"Julian's first Town Hall was privately owned and stood on the corner of Main Street and Washington." according to James Jasper. *"It was a flimsy affair hastily constructed of 16-foot rough boards and contained a bar. A violent windstorm in 1872 wrecked the building and it was not rebuilt."*

"The second Hall was also privately owned and known as Morris Hall. It was a pretentious rustic affair built of pine logs and slabs and stood on Main Street on a lot now (1934) occupied by the A.P. Frary residence. Later it was turned into a saloon.

"The third Hall was a public building erected by subscription on a lot donated by D.D. Bailey near where the Washington Hotel (in block 9) now stands. The town outgrew the building and it was disposed of at public auction to D.D. Bailey. It was built in 1876 to celebrate the Centennial by the miners and saw mill owners in one week.

PUBLISHED BY JAMES A. JASPER

P. O. Box 316   SAN DIEGO, CALIFORNIA

JULIAN TOWN HALL

◉∾ LEADING FEATURES ∾◉

Julian and Surroundings	GEO. P. HALL
Christmas Thoughts	JOHN COLLIS MOORE
Recreation Pointers	A. D. JORDAN
Aquatic Sports	DR. T. G. McCONKEY
Mothers' Club Department	Edited by MRS. J. WAGNER HAVICE

Illustrations, Poet's Corner, and Miscellaneous Matters of Interest.

Price, $1.00 per Year
Single Copy, 10 Cents

December, 1899

THE JULIAN HOTEL stood where the present Town Hall now stands on the corner of Washington and Main. It was built in 1872 by George Hoskings and burned to the ground about 1900. This picture was taken about 1885 and shows a four horse stage starting its run to San Diego. About this time Peter Meyerhofer was hotel proprietor and also ran a brewery located in the building which presently houses the Julian Historical Museum.

JULIAN'S "PRETENTIOUS" TOWN HALL (facing page) was featured in this turn of the century edition of James Jasper's "The Silver Gate" magazine. Jasper had moved to San Diego to assume the duties of a County Supervisor, at the same time pursuing is journalism profession. He was so good as a San Diego County booster that the chamber of commerce hired him to travel around the nation promoting the region at major fairs and conventions.

"The fourth Hall was a public, pretentious building costing over $6,000. and occupied a corner on Main and B Streets. The Hall burned down in 1912."

"Thus we see," noted Jasper in 1934, *"Julian has suffered much loss in the many disastrous fires, and much valuable information has been destroyed."*

The fifth and present Hall was built in 1914 and still stands today on the corner of Main and Washington Streets. It occupies the same site as the former Julian Hotel which also was consumed by fire.

In 1913, Julian realized they couldn't go for long without a town hall and set out to raise private subscriptions to build a new one. It was only a matter of a few months before $4,500 was pledged. The new structure had both main floor and basement halls, complete with *"gents' and ladies' rest and toilet rooms".* It also boasted *"two separate lighting plants, one above and one below, and would be a credit to a much larger town than Julian",* so stated the Ramona Sentinel of August 28, 1914. The whole project came in under budget for a total cost of $3,136, much to the credit of the building committee.

UNSCRUPULOUS SALOON KEEPER

It was said that Charley Hale ran the toughest joint in Julian. Not satisfied with fleecing the drinking and gambling miners and Indians, he robbed them as well.

One summer day, two Indians from the Mategui rancheria came to town and fell victim to Hale's greed. *"Not content with the pittance of their purses,"* Jasper related, *"he induced one of them to sell him his pony, then robbed him of the purchase price. Having made his cleanup, Hale stabled the pony and went his way to dinner, when, 'lo, the poor Indian went to the stable, mounted the pony and made his getaway. When the theft - if theft it can be called - was discovered, Hale swore out a complaint charging the Indians with grand larceny, a warrant was issued for their arrest and I was dispatched to bring in the culprits."*

In addition to running the town's newspaper, Jasper, was constable and deputy sheriff at the time of this incident.

"I overhauled one of the Indians in Ballena and lodged him in jail before night but the one on the stolen pony had made his getaway. Learning from my captive that the other Indian lived at the Mategui," Jasper continued, "I made my way to the rancheria the next morning and demanded the surrender of the Indian, but the Capitano denied any knowledge of his where-abouts."

Having recognized the stolen pony grazing nearby I was not to be put off with such denial and after a prolonged search found my man under the bed in an old adobe on the outskirts of the rancheria and hauled him out feet foremost. The Capitano furiously protested my right to remove the Indian from the Reservation, and not until after an effective gun-play was I permitted to depart with my captive, and then six bucks mounted their ponies and followed me 20 miles to Julian, never letting me out of their pistol range."

Ballena attorney J.P. Tucker appeared for the Indians when the case came up and his first move was for a change of venue. The motion was granted and the case transferred to the Mesa Grande Judicial Township. At that time each Judicial Township in San Diego County was entitled to two Justices of the Peace. At the election preceding this case there was only one candidate for judge in Mesa Grande, Nester A. Young. Someone wrote in the name of William Halleran as a joke.

"Well," continued Jasper, *"the joke was on the joker, for Halleran qualified; that made Young so mad, he refused to qualify, and left Mesa Grande with a judge who knew nothing of court procedure or law. About a week after the transcript was forwarded I received through the mail the following notice:*

"Mr. Constable Julian:
   Your injuns will be tried at the school house friday.
               Wm. Halleran, J.P."

No date, no township. My official responsibility having ceased with the transfer of the case, I ignored the notice other than passing it on to Hale the complainant, who on advice of his attorney, also ignored it. When the case came up in Holleran's court, there were no prosecuting witnesses, and the Judge, not knowing how to proceed, asked Tucker what he should do. "Discharge the prisoners and fine the constable the cost of the suit", said Tucker, and it was so ordered. Another week went by and the mail brought me another notice, to wit:

"Mr. Constable Julian:
   I discharged your injuns and fined you the cost $6.00 send money at once and save trouble.
               Wm. Halleran, J.P."

"It may be of interest to note here that Hale never recovered his pony, nor did Judge Halleran receive his six dollars, the constable forgot to send it. After numerous threats of attachment suits, the Judge made a special trip to the County Seat to enlist the aid of James Copeland, District Attorney; but Copeland laughed him out of his office. That was the first and last case of Judge Halleran. He was so disgusted with his failure to collect that six dollars that he resigned his office.

In the meantime Tucker got busy and filed a complaint in the Federal Court at Los Angeles charging Hale with selling whisky to the Indians; he was arrested, tried before Judge Wellborn and the verdict proved the truth of the

CONVENTION GATHERING While we've been unable to determine the event or date, this photo is believed to be taken at a gathering of San Diego County constables. (front row, 1 to r) Charlie Kelly, Cho Stanley, James George, Lute (Luther) Bailey, ? Echeverry. (top row) Charlie Bailey, Tom Stanley, Eurat Sawday, Frank Harriet, Bob Walker and Clarance King.

adage "Ill gotten gains are dearly bought". For retribution came at last when the Judge sentenced Hale to serve six months in jail and pay a fine of five hundred dollars.

"I was subpoenaed as a witness in the case but was not called to the stand. I was informed at headquarters that the complaining witnesses (Indians) got beastly drunk in Los Angeles as soon as they received their witness fees, and could not find the depot to go home, and had to be put on the train by a government official."

When James Jasper arrived on the Julian scene, during the late 1880s, the town was pretty much being run by the saloon owners. One was *"Justice of the Peace and another one Constable. Court was held in the saloon, and*

AUGUST GRAND (right) served as Deputy Sheriff of Julian for about 30 years, from 1926 until 1956. Shown here with J,eff Swycaffer, son of Ballena pioneer settler Joe. Jeff wasn't a constable or deputy sheriff but usually dressed the part, complete with side-arm even when visiting the big city. Grand's district went as far as Riverside and Imperial County lines.

the rough element was conceded the right-of-way, and they took advantage of the situation." Jasper related. Soon after a few too many unsavory incidents happened, however, *"the better element of the community got busy and induced the Justice and the Constable to resign and petitioned the Board of Supervisors to appoint F.E. Van Houten, Justice and the writer (Jasper) Constable and Deputy Sheriff."*

The appointments were made, and thus began yet another career for the venerable Jasper,

11

Changing Scene

The town center Drue Bailey laid out was a lively place during the 1870s and early 1880s. Despite the stultifying effect the grant boundary fight had on its settlers, the town supported a variety of business enterprises.

According to James Jasper, *"Joseph Swycaffer was the man of the hour; he started the first store and butcher shop, bringing in supplies over a trail through Kanaka Flat. As to who started the first saloon, camp historians differ, but all agree they were there in plenty, and thirst was unknown in Julian prior to the eighteenth amendment."*... *"boose flowed freely and revelry ran high."*

Julian City had eight saloons. There were also five stores, two hotels, two cafes, two livery stables and two blacksmith shops in the early 1870s.

Soon after the big discoveries down in San Felipe Canyon, the town of Banner City blossomed adding an additional two stores, one hotel and three saloons to the mountain scene.

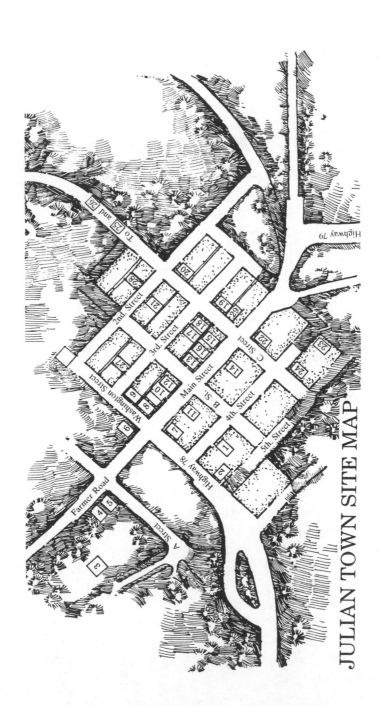

KEY TO JULIAN TOWN SITE MAP
Historical Use and Present Use

1. Witch Creek School
   Julian Library Today
2. Mayerhofer Brewery
   Treshil Blacksmith Shop
   Julian Historical Museum Today
3. Haven of Rest Cemetary
4. Taylor/Bailey Residence
   Residence Today
5. J.C. Silvers Store
   Restaurant Today
6. Jacoby General Store
   Grocery Store Today
7. Julian Hotel
   Julian Town Hall Today
8. A. Levi & Co./
   Joseph Marks Mercantile
   Julian Drug Store Today
9. Joseph Marks Residence
   Antique Store Today
10. Swycaffer Saloon
    Daley Butcher Store
    Liquor Store Today
11. F.A. DeLuca Genl. Store
    Jack's Grocery Store Today
12. Wilcox/F.L. Blanc
    General Store
    Sprague Realty Today
13. Robinson Bakery/Restaurant
    Robinson Hotel
    Julian Hotel Today
14. A.P. Frary Jr. Residence
    Retail Shop Today

15. Thos. Daley Rental
    Retail Store Today
16. F.A. Deluca Residence
    Restaurant Today
17. F.L. Blanc Rental
    Residence today
18. F.L. Blanc Residence
    Church Building Today
19. F.L. Blanc Rental
    Residence Today
20. Baptist Church Parsonage
    Bed & Breakfast Inn Today
21. Julian Elementary School
    Apartments Today

22. Thomas Strick Residence
    Residence Today
23. Cuyamaca Union High School
    Apartments and Retail Today
24. County Jail
    Historical Exhibit Today
25. George Washington Mine
    Historical Exhibit Today
26. Eagle/High Peak Mine
    Museum and Mine Tours Today
27. Clarence King Residence
    Residential and Retail Today
28. Unidentified Residence
29. F.L. Blanc Warehouse
    Julian Women's Club Today

It's believed that Hale & Porter's Saloon, and the Julian Sentinel shared the building site next to where the Julian Drug Store is today.

Map from *Design Guidelines Manual, Julian Historic District,*
Published by County of San Diego, Department of Planning and Land Use,

TEN CENT TOKEN, good for one "hooker" of whiskey at Joe Swycaffer's Julian Saloon. Circa 1870s.

But by 1889, competition for Julian's shrinking commercial trade had whittled the number of stores down to three and blacksmith shops and livery stables down to one each. However, one newspaper and one barber shop had been added to the scene. The town still had two hotels and seven saloons where, according to Jasper, *"200 miners of the camp gathered every day in the year to drink and gamble and many were the reckless miners who parted with their payroll at the gaming tables."*

According to ads running in the Julian Sentinel during the early 1890s, *"The Chief Saloon - was located opposite the Sentinel office in Julian"* and featured *"Choice Wines, Liquors & Cigars, C.W. Hale - Proprietor."*

A visitor to back country in the late nineteenth century had a choice of several hotels and boarding houses. The Julian Hotel's 1890 advertisement stated *"The table will be supplied with the best the Market affords and the Comfort of Guests will be our first consideration. Board & Lodging per week $7.00, Board per week, $6.00 and Board per day $1.00. No Chinese Cooks Employed! Peter Mayrhofer, manager."*

VIEW FROM A HILL looking south over Julian at the turn of the century. In the center, Town Hall dominates Main Street. Down a block, to the right, stood the Julian Hotel before it burned down. Present Town Hall occupies that site today. North Cuyamaca Peak can be seen through the haze in the background.

There was also the *"Mt. View Hotel - Main Street Julian. New Building, elegantly furnished. Rates $7 to $9 per week. Henry Garland, Prop."*

A stage passenger to San Diego in the 1890s had his chance to stop along the way and enjoy the hospitality of such as the Ramona Hotel. According to their ad in the Sentinel, it was *"a large brick, well furnished & well kept house. The table will be supplied with the best the market affords, Rate by month $25.00, by the week $7.00 and by the day $1.25. - Half way between Foster & Julian."* The Ramona Hotel was built in 1887 by Milton Santee as part of the Santa Maria Land and Water Company's land sales promotion program.

It was later renamed the Kennelworth Inn and expanded to two stories in 1915 by its new owner, H.A. Miles who hoped to attract visitors coming to the Panama-Pacific Exposition in San Diego. Located on the northwest corner of Eighth and Main Streets, it was a popular spot right up until it burned down in 1943

Two items from the May 10, 1894 edition of the Ramona Sentinel:

"The new brick store of A. Levi & Co. is about ready for the tin roof, and is a very handsome building. Mr. Perry of your city (San Diego) is the contractor"

The building referred to in that item still stands today and has been the Julian Drug Store since the early 1930s. Before then, it was the Joseph Marks Mercantile store.

"One of the old land marks of Julian, The Chief saloon, is being torn down this week to be replaced by a billiard saloon 16x24 feet, for J.D. Rush. The old building was built in Banner in 1875 and hauled up to Julian and erection on its present site. It has seen all our ups and downs, witnessed the palmy days of our several so-called booms and survived several periods of depression and has done duty in its time as saloon, boarding house, warehouse, dwelling and workshop."

In reading this item, doesn't it make you wonder how those old western movies portraying the typical gold boom-town saloon might have fit Julian. Their big ornate bars with expansive crystal mirrors and bar-keeps with white aprons, several tables of poker in progress, interrupted by an occasional brawl resulting in bodies flying off the balconies, chairs crashing into the aforementioned mirrors and a sheriff swaggering onto the scene through double swinging doors with six-

BASEBALL TEAM Julian's ball team, about 1910. Spirited rivalry existed between Julian and such back country towns as Escondido, Poway and Ramona. Uniforms and equipment appear to be first-class for those days, especially when compared with that seen in pictures of the Ramona and Poway teams of the same era. Maybe some rich mine owner sponsored the Julian team. Shown kneeling are Luther Bailey, (son of town father Drue), left and Mr. Powers. Standing left to right: Ray Detrick, Hardy Ford, unknown, Lon Smith, unknown, Leland Wellington, Bob Haley, Claude Swycaffer, Rex Detrick, John Campbell and Roy Stephens.

shooters aimed at the wrong-doers.

Guess that scene wouldn't fit Julian. Hollywood couldn't have squeezed all that scenery and action into the Chief's 24 foot wide building.

JULIAN'S BREWERY

That Julian had a brewery is evident from the building that still stands today and currently serves as the local history museum. The Julian Historical Society tells us the brewer was a fellow named Peter Mayerhoffer. Peter was also the proprietor of the Julian Hotel a block north.

The brewery operated from about 1885, when it was built, until about 1888. But as to what kind of suds were produced, and how much, no one seems to know. The building was sold to Joseph Treshil, a blacksmith and remained a blacksmith shop until into the 1930s. It has been a museum since the 1950s.

SOME DEMOGRAPHICS

The big gold rush in the winter and spring of 1870, brought a divergent mass of humanity to San Diego County's Cuyamaca mountains.

It is interesting, and fortunate from a historian's standpoint, that the U.S. Federal decennial census for 1870 was scheduled to take place at the height of the boom that very summer. While the census taker in those days asked very few questions, compared with today, the answers are interesting never the less.

From July 10th through the 16th, the census enumerator picked his way through the tents and shacks that dotted the local landscape in an attempt to count all the people in the Julian District of San Diego County.

Like most other mining camps in their boom times, Julian had its share of rapscallions and ne'er-do-wells. Mining camps attracted all types. But for the most part, the men and women he found had brought skills and trades that contributed to the establishment of a new settlement. Most were bent on improving their lot in life, and gold mining seemed to offer more rewards than what they'd been doing. Many of them came from the eastern part of our young nation.

In those days questions to be answered on the standard

census form were few and to the point. Under "occupation" the census taker was looking for the person's current pursuit. So its not surprising to find that "gold miner" topped the list. These raw entries, however, don't tell us what other skills or previous experience the miner respondent possessed or level of his education. But an analysis of the responses listed reflects a population cross section that was fairly self sufficient. (See Appendix A)

Its been generally thought the young town was predominately populated by southerners. While it's true Julian City was founded by Drury Bailey and named for Mike Julian, both Georgia natives, an analysis of that census paints a different picture of the town's typical settler and miner of that day.

The largest block, 37% of the adults, were born in the northern and eastern part of the U.S. The next largest group, 29% were foreign born, with a third of those coming from Ireland. Southern born adults accounted for 27% of the young town's population, while the balance, 7.5% were from border states.

Those who listed their occupation as gold miner typically were living as single men who called a bedroll, or at best a tent, home.

Julian City was a melting pot of races, nationalities and religions. The Irish constituted the majority of foreign born, while Canadians, English, Scotchmen and Germans were prevalent.

But a number of black people contributed to Julian's history. Fred Coleman was the first, and the creek from which the gold strike was made, starting off the Julian boom, was named for him. Coleman was from the northern California gold fields, and is said to have known gold when he saw it.

Also prominent in the community were the Robinsons,

ROBINSON RESTAURANT AND BAKERY pictured about the turn of the century. The building was torn down to make way for the Robinson Hotel. Margaret Tull Robinson is presumed to be the woman shown in front of the others. The present Julian Hotel occupies the site today.

Albert and Margaret Tull. They were outstanding cooks and build a little bakery and restaurant business into a successful hotel. Originally named the Robinson, today it is called the Julian Hotel. Albert was a former slave who came to San Diego soon after the Civil War with Major Chase, who was his former master.

J. Green was another respected black pioneer. He worked for Drury Bailey in the Julian livery stable in the mid-1870s. A hard-working, independent man who was

AMERICA NEWTON was one of Julian's more colorful characters. Highly respected as a person and for the fine laundry work she did for her customers. Pictured here about 1910, she was the proud owner of an 80 acre homestead 2 miles west of Julian near Spencer Valley.

known for being as "honest as the day is long", it was said he was thrifty, often lending money to needy white folks.

Many Chinese workers, who had recently finished work on Central Pacific Railroad construction drifted into the area in search of work. When they found it, it generally was the most menial of tasks and their living quarters, the worst. Other miners resented their presence, and it wasn't uncommon for some to be killed in fights. Julian had a Chinese laundry which was an accepted part of that pioneer community and did well for several years.

While they had it rough, most were resilient and shrewd. Many returned to China with substantial savings.

In 1887 a large group of Chinese laborers helped build

THE LAST HOTEL IN JULIAN to carry the town's name, as it appears today. It was originally established as the Robinson Hotel, and has since been expanded. (See picture opposite page)

the San Diego Flume. It ran from the bottom of Boulder Creek for 37 miles into east San Diego. (More about that later). Tunnels had to be dug as well as footings for the flume's trestles. Many thousands of cubic yards of dirt and rock were moved by collies in those days before bulldozers.

JULIAN CHURCHES

The Julian Community Baptist Church is the oldest religious organization to conduct continuous services in the town. This congregation had its beginning in 1885 when Reverend Thomas Jackson Wood conducted services in the Town Hall in September that year.

Rev. Wood had come from London England to the Ballena Valley in 1884 to tudor three Sawday boys and serve as minister for the surrounding country.

ROBINSON HOTEL about 1912. This building formed the basic structure of the Julian Hotel of today. The name was changed in 1918.

Wood received a call to preach in Julian and the first meeting, which was held at the Town Hall, drew an overflow crowd. The American Baptist Home Missionary recognized the unmet need for services in the back country and engaged Reverend Wood as a full time missionary for the area from Ballena to Julian and Mesa Grande to Palomar with a salary $100. But the area he had to cover was so big that he was able to come to Julian but once a month.

The growing congregation needed a church building and, true to his word, Drue Bailey donated two lots to get the project started. The first meeting was held in that new Baptist Church in December 1891. A full time minister was hired, the Reverend Frank L. Blanc who held that position for 27 years.

After 70 years of service, the original church building was razed in 1960 and replaced with a new one in 1961. Thus, the Baptist church of Julian, which started in the Town Hall, and has seen construction of two new buildings, can lay claim to being Julian's oldest congregation with over 106 years of continuous service in the community.

Other religious congregations conducting regular services in Julian include the Catholic Church, the Methodist Church and the Church of Jesus Christ of Latter Day Saints. While the other three congregations now meet in their own church buildings, the newly formed Mormon group is meeting in temporary quarters and have plans for building a church soon.

The Roman Catholic Church has had a presence in our back country for over two centuries, but it wasn't until the mid-1900s that the first permanent church building was built in Julian. St. Elizabeth was formally dedicated by Bishop Charles F. Buddy in October 1949. Except for a fire in 1962 that burned the interior of the church and closed it for a brief time, the congregation has met there continuously for nearly a half century.

The Julian Community United Methodist Church was formed in June 1963. After six years of meeting in temporary quarters, funds were raised and the current church built in 1969.

12

The Flume

The big southern California land rush of the late 1880s was in full swing and San Diego County was very much a part of the boom.

But it had become clear to those with foresight, that outside sources of water would be needed if semi-desert San Diego was to sustain its rapid growth rate. The few wells that existed in the burgeoning city couldn't keep pace with demand. The dam the Padres had built in what is known today as Mission Gorge was being put to good use by the City, but bigger and bolder improvements would be needed to keep pace with exploding demands.

By 1881, most of the promising dam sites in San Diego County had been identified. A leader in this effort was local civil engineer and water development pioneer, T.S. Van Dyke. One of the more likely spots he found was located just 40 miles east of the growing city, in the Cuyamaca Mountains. This is where the snows fell in the winter and where rains could build needed reserves of precious water.

Van Dyke visualized a system that would collect this mountain water with a series of dams, and deliver it by way of extensive flumes and aqueducts to San Diego and the intervening potential farm lands that would later become Lemon Grove, LaMesa and Spring Valley.

Before such a vast system could become reality, however, large sums of money would have to be raised, millions of cubic yards of dirt moved and millions of board feet of redwood timber fabricated and installed.

As it developed, one of Van Dyke's good hunting friends, William E. Robinson became the catalyst for raising the necessary capital, Chinese coolies moved the dirt and rock and skilled carpenters cut, fit and erected the 36 miles of redwood trestle and flume.

In November 1885, news broke of the Santa Fe Railroad's purchase of a 242 mile rail link assuring San Diego of direct transcontinental service. This was all that Van Dyke and Robinson needed to know the time was finally right for their ambitious plans. San Diego's population was soon bound to swell beyond what existing water supplies could service.

The two set about to refine their plans for the water system and for organizing a company to make it a reality. The San Diego Flume Company was at long last formed on May 27, 1886. The organizers included A. W. Hawley, wealthy real estate man from the El Cajon Valley, George D. Copeland, G. Frank Judson, W. H. Somers, Van Dyke and Robinson.

The master plan called for two dams, plus a wooden flume and series of tunnels. The main dam would be located in the west end of Cuyamaca Valley near the old Stonewall Mine. This site formed a natural basin. In the winter when the valley was saturated, water ran "through the pass of Cosear (between the second and third ridges)

T.S. VAN DYKE, father of one of the country's more spectacular water works projects, the San Diego Flume. Shown here about 1910 at his Daggett ranch.

into the San Diego River".

The Mexicans knew this site before Americans came as "La Laguna que se Seca", (the lagoon that dries up). That is the name that appeared on Don Olvera's diseño for the Rancho Cuyamaca. This same valley was the site of the ancient Indian villages of Cuyamaca and Yguai.

In the summer of 1870, when the gold rush was in full swing, about 2,000 head of cattle, along with horse stock were grazing there.

The plan was for water to flow down Boulder Creek from the main reservoir to a second dam located in the San Diego River below. From there, water would be carried by flume to the western outskirts of San Diego.

In acquiring the main reservoir site, however, the flume promoters attempted to by pass the legal owner of the land. They figured they could get the necessary land through condemnation. Laws of eminent domain in those days apparently were looser and the organizers felt that since they were providing a public service, land acqusition was one expense they needn't be burdened with.

The owner of the land, Governor Robert W. Waterman didn't see it that way, nor did he take it lightly when he heard that some of his finer grazing land was slated to become lake bottom. When he pressed his point, the flume company filed suit in San Diego Superior court in October 1887 for condemnation rights to 600 acres of Waterman's land. The Governor's main concern was the expansion of the lake and the proposed reservoir's effect on his Stonewall mine operations. The mine's lead consisted of a nearly perpendicular crevice filled with gold bearing quartz. The strike, or course of the crevice, passed under the effected land and could be rendered worthless if it became flooded through percolation.

Waterman petitioned the court for a change in venue, claiming he couldn't get a fair trial where the citizens of San Diego were strongly in favor of a new water system. He lost his request and immediately appealed to the State Supreme Court There he was turned down as well.

Waterman sought $100,000 for damages to the mine and another $110,000 for land acquisition and damages. But when it became clear the cards were stacked against him, he agreed to negotiate, and ultimately settled for $45,000. $20,000 was paid at time of signing with the balance to be paid over a 10 year period, interest at 10% per annum. This was to compensate him for his land. Nothing was paid for possible damage to his mine. But he did obtain rights to use the road across the dam, as well as rights for boating, fishing and hunting on the lake. The agreement also contained a clause that should the Flume Company use the land for other than a reservoir, it would revert back to the Watermans.

Any acrimony caused by the skirmish over the reservoir site, apparently had been smoothed over by the time the flume was dedicated in February 1889. Governor Waterman was an honored guest during the two day celebration and rode in the front seat of the lead boat down the completed flume.

But before they could celebrate, a tremendous amount of construction was completed in little over two years; a very short time considering it was all done by man and horse. No big bull-dozers in those days.

To create the main Cuyamaca Lake reservoir a dam 720 feet long and 35 feet high was erected. Design called for an earthen structure over a rock shelf. As it developed, however, the shelf was clay, not rock, and 1,500 barrels of cement had to be used for reinforcement. The dam survives today, pretty much as it was originally built over 100 years ago. Only minor changes have since been made to meet modern safety standards, in 1950 and again in 1982, when new spillway structures were added.

When full, the lake covers 900 acres with a design capacity of 3.7 billion gallons of water.

From this reservoir, water fell down Boulder Creek about twelve miles to a second, diverting dam. That 400 foot long dam, built of masonry, was the point from which the flume began. From that point, in the upper reaches of the San Diego River, to its terminus eight miles east of the city proper, the flume stretched 35.6 miles.

The flume was built to an even grade of four feet, eight inches fall to the mile. There were over three hundred and fifteen trestles and numerous cuts and tunnels. In order to avoid washouts and slides, no earth fill was allowed. Where native rock or firm earth was not at the proper height, a trestle strong enough to support

CHINESE COOLIES provided the power to excavate thousands of cubic yards of rock and dirt. No fill-dirt was used to achieve the fall of four feet, eight inches to the mile required for the flume. The constant grade was maintained by building trestles and digging tunnels.

a locomotive, was built to maintain the grade. A small army of Chinese collies followed close on surveyor's stakes, shoveling away dirt and rock.

The echo and re-echo of black powder blasts shattering boulders and solid rock, the scraping of coolies' shovels and the incessant noise of carpenters' hammers, must have presented some unaccustomed sights and sounds to the many deer and other wild animals in this previously undisturbed setting.

Nine million board feet of lumber was used to complete the flume. It was six feet wide and sixteen inches high, built of clear redwood planks two inches thick which rested on mud sills, stringers and cross ties.

Some of the trestles supporting it were truly impressive: The Sweetwater Pass, 1,264 feet long and 81 feet high; Sweetwater Pass #2, 2,720 feet long and 25 feet high; Los Coches, 1,774 feet long and 65 feet high

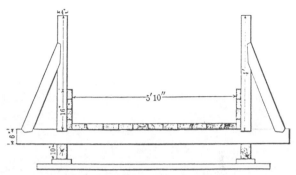

ONLY CLEAR-HEART REDWOOD was used in the flume's construction. The bench style flume was 6 feet wide and planked with boards 2 inches thick. Nine million board of lumber was used to build the 36 mile long structure.

and the Sycamore Creek, 720 feet long and 35 feet high, to name a few. Two tunnels over 400 feet long were dug which required much blasting powder and coolie labor.

Over one hundred wagons, with eight hundred horses and mules, transported the timber that had been prefabricated in San Diego. Caravans of eight to ten team wagons would wind their way up the mountains over special roads constructed at great expense.

The precious water the flume brought from the Cuyamaca Mountains made it possible for east county to develop and blossom. And the San Diego Flume Company didn't confine its energies to selling water. In the early 1890s, they were selling land in the La Mesa Colony. They offered ten acre parcels with water entitlements of one miner's inch (12,960 gallons) of water per day per parcel for $100 per acre. Their ad chided, however, that if the purchaser was not interested in the water, he could have the land for $15 an acre.

San Diego County experienced a prolonged drought at the turn of the century. From 1900 to 1904 the Cuyamaca reservoir site was dry and the whole area was planted in hay.

THIS TRESTLE crossed Los Coches Creek east of El Cajon. It was a third of a mile long and 65 feet high.

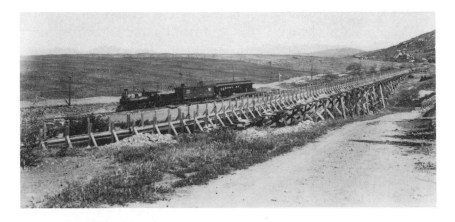

SAN DIEGO CUYAMACA AND EASTERN RR tracks ran along side the flume through the eastern part of El Cajon Valley. This 1890s picture was taken just north of present Interstate 8 and east of today's Grossmont Center.

LIKE CAULKING A SHIP'S DECK 36 MILES LONG. This is what these men had to do to make the newly constructed flume water-tight. After many years of caulking and driving wedges the company finally gave up and lined it with tarpaper to keep maintenace costs down.

In order to meet their obligations to furnish water to the farmers and orchardists during the drought, the flume company was forced to drill wells and pump water from the El Monte Basin. In 1904 the bond holders were forced to take over and operate the company. In 1910 James Murray and Ed Fletcher bought the San Diego Flume Company. They later renamed it the Cuyamaca Water Company.

But with the explosive growth that came to San Diego during World War I, the City was once again searching for more water. Capturing more of the great water resources of the Cuyamaca and Laguna Mountains would be necessary and that required much larger dams.

It was determined that a dam built on the San Diego River next to El Capitan Mountain would impound much of the water flowing down the various water courses into the San Diego River basin. When plans for

WATER : RIGHTS !

——OF——

ONE MINER'S INCH TO EACH TRACT,

Are deeded with every ten-acre tract in LA MESA COL-
ONY, sold by the San Diego Flume Company, the
water being PIPED UNDER PRESSURE through the colony.
This WATER RIGHT IS PERPETUAL and it entitles the
tract to 12,960 gallons of water every 24 hours!

These tracts, with the water right, are now being sold
at $100 per acre, and as La Mesa is on the Frostless
Fruit Belt, only a short distance from this city, with
the Cuyamaca railroad running four trains each day
through it, the property is being rapidly picked up by
orange and lemon growers and suburban home-seekers.
Land is PLENTIFUL all over the county, but land with a
PERPETUAL WATER RIGHT IS VERY SCARCE. If you
wish to farm for PROFIT you MUST HAVE a water right
with your land. However, if you want to try it without a water right, we will sell you good La Mesa lands
without water for $15 an acre.

These prices challenge the attention of all who intend purchasing fruit lands, and they also challenge
competition, and invite the most thorough investigation
of the property.

FOR FURTHER PARTICULARS, CALL ON OR ADDRESS

SAN DIEGO FLUME COMPANY,
Rooms 19 and 20, Consolidated Bank Building.

THE FLUME COMPANY OWNED VAST TRACTS of land in La Mesa
and used their water to help sell property. The above advertisement ran in the
April 2, 1891 edition of the Daily San Diegan. It was flume water that helped
establish the lush orchards and town of La Mesa in the 1890s. But alas the
drought of 1900-03 dried up Lake Cuyamaca and the company was forced to
drill wells in the El Cajon Valley to fullfill their water obligations.

OPENING DAY CELEBRATION for the new flume. Sitting on the right in the front seat of the first boat, was Governor Waterman, despite the fact the flume promotors had initially tried to steal his land for their main reservoir.

the new dam were being finalized in 1919, it became clear that the flume would become history. Its water rights would be preempted and much of its right of way, as well the Eagle Peak Road blocked by the newly created reservoir.

The flume had been in place less than 30 years when plans to make it obsolete were drafted in 1916. But it took 17 years from the time those wheels were set in motion until "El Cap" was finished in the early 1930s. Those years were filled with intense political and legal battles. One battle was over Indian land rights, the other over the flume company's water rights.

The City of San Diego claimed rights over all water flowing in the San Diego River. Since Boulder Creek, and Cuyamaca Lake were tributaries of that river they were included in the City's claim. The court's decision finally turned on a legal point going back to Spain's occupation of California. San Diego had been planned as a pueblo by the Spanish and under Spanish law, pueblos had paramount rights over all water flowing through them. Murray and Fletcher had to settle for $600,000 for their rights, and the flume company was history.

The Capitan Grande Indian Reservation covered the floor of the vast San Diego River basin where the new lake was to be created. As it developed, the Indian's interests were dealt with and settled in a relatively short time with enactment of the "Capitan Grande Reservoir Act of 1919." This bill was introduced and carried by local Congressman William Kettner and paved the way for the City of San Diego to buy the Indian's land so they could purchase new reservation lands and establish new homes. This ultimately resulted in the formation of the Barona and Viejas Reservations where most of the tribe moved in 1933.

Willis Fletcher, son of Col. Ed, recently told the author of his experiences with the flume. During the summer of 1923, as a student of 18, "Wig", (as he is called by friends) lived in Lakeside and worked on the maintenance of the ever-leaking flume. Some of the planks would dry out in spots causing the seams to open. Wig's job was to carry a large sack of wedges. These wedges were driven between the planks and uprights by a "big Swede" with a sledge hammer, thus cinching the loose boards tighter and slowing down the leaks, somewhat. *"Seems that rattlesnakes liked the cool, damp spots in the shade of the flume,"* according to Willis, *"and*

*one day one of them struck at the sack of wedges and just
about scared me to death. My boss, the "Swede" took care
of him in short order. It was an experience I never forgot."*

But alas, the wedge method of keeping the boards tight
finally gave way to a less labor intensive solution. The
flume was ultimately lined with tar paper, and that's the
way it was in its final days.

With the El Capitan Dam finalized, and the San Diego
river dammed northeast of Lakeside, the venerable old
flume was history. It had served the people well, but its
capacity limitations, high maintenance costs and the
City's determination to preempt its water, rendered it
obsolete. Much more water could be stored behind a
giant dam like "El Cap" and distribution of water
through underground pipe was more practical.

For the 45 or so years it lived, however, the great
Cuyamaca Flume opened opportunities for new farms
and orchards, providing life giving water to a rapidly
growing east county.

One last question - you ask what happened to all that
beautiful clear-heart redwood timber that came from
dismantling the flume? We can only assume that much
of it wound up in a lot of east county houses during the
great depression of the 1930s.

What remains of the old system today are the main
reservoir, Lake Cuyamaca, the diverting dam, where
Boulder Creek converges with the San Diego River and
some sections of open concrete culvert that has
weathered the 100 years since it was poured.

Lake Cuyamaca became part of the Helix Irrigation
District. From the mid-1930s until 1968, it was the
District's practice to withdraw water from the lake about
May 1st each year. This left the basin dry during the
summer and fall until the winter rains refilled it, and for
about thirty years it was closed to the public.

WILLIS FLETCHER, conservationist, businessman and son of Col Ed Fletcher, former owner of the flume company. Shown here in 1991 at his home on the base of North Peak overlooking Lake Cuyamaca.

But in 1961 and 1963 local sportsmen got the California Legislature to enact bills which created the Cuyamaca Recreation and Parks District and provided it with authority to operate and fund the district.

Working with grant-in-aid from the Wildlife Conservation Board of the State Department of Fish and Game the new district was able to construct improvements. These included a water retention dike, water transfer pumping facilities, parking lots, sanitary facilities and docks.

Finally in the summer of 1968 the lake was again opened to fishing and duck hunting.

13

Apples

While the search for gold remained high on the agenda for many who came to Julian in the nineteenth century, there were others who early on recognized the great agricultural potential of the area. One of these was James Madison who arrived in San Diego from New York in 1867 in search of suitable land to raise horses.

Madison settled for a portion of Cuyamaca grantland, in the area of present day Pine Hills. There he developed the Shilo breed of horses. He also quickly saw that the climate, soil and elevation would lend itself to apple growing.

It is popularly believed that Madison and Thomas Brady went to central California in the early 1870s and brought back the first wagon load of apple trees to the region. Other early pioneers in apple orchard planting were Isaac Bush, David Talley, Henry Morris, L.N. Bailey, Chester Gunn and James Duffy.

While gold mining activity in the area was either boom or bust, and mostly bust as time went by, cultivation of apples grew steadily, becoming the mainstay and economic savior of Julian.

The San Diego Union reported in its November 11, 1880 edition: *"James Madison who has produced 600 pounds of large and juicy Bellflowers from a single tree, is this season putting in 175 acres of wheat."* The writer went on to say, *"The agricultural mines on top of the ground, and the mineral mines beneath will all yield a golden harvest this year, and every acre will do more towards promoting a genuine "prosperity" for San Diego County and City than all the "real estate booms" that can be concocted between this and doomsday."*

In 1889, the California legislature passed an enabling act and appropriated $2,000 to provide for formation of a San Diego County District Fair. The District was promptly organized and the first fair held in Escondido the following year. There was a $50 silk banner hung up for the best community display which became the property of the town that won it three successive times. A $60 riding cultivator was also awarded for the best community display.

The District Fair competition generated considerable enthusiasm in the various small towns in the County. James Jasper wrote in the Julian Sentinel: *"That banner would look fine floating from a pine tree here in the mountains, and in order to settle all disputes Julian would descend from her lofty perch and bring it home."* The comment created quite a stir with other County papers which printed it, lambasting Jasper for his audacity.

With Jasper's leadership and drive, however, a large assortment of Julian fruit was indeed assembled and a display set-up at the fair. Julian won the banner, the cultivator and 88 first and second prizes. In later years, Jasper's promotional skills led him to resign his seat on the County Board of Supervisors to accept a position to

CHESTER GUNN'S FARM pictured here about 1885, was the site of one of Julian's earliest apple orchards.

travel throughtout the United States promoting San Diego for the Chamber of Commerce.

Julian apples' fame spread as area farmers started shipping their produce around the country and exhibiting in various county, state and world fairs.

Lula Juch, widow of Arthur Juch, was interviewed in her Julian home in 1956 by Edgar Hastings of the San Diego Historical Society. According to Mrs Juch, *"Apples were displayed and took blue ribbons and first prizes at the World's Fair in Chicago in 1893, the St. Louis Fair - Norfolk Virginia - Watsonville and the San Francisco Word's Fair of 1915. Her husband," she added, "was chosen by the Julian farmers to exhibit at these fairs."*

Such old time apple men as L.W. (Bud) Farmer, considers Arthur Juch was one of Julian's most progressive apple pioneers. *"He was twenty five years*

BUY A BOX OF JULIAN APPLES"—A FINE ASSORTMENT WILL BE ON EXHIBIT AND FOR SALE IN RAMONA, SATURDAY, NOVEMBER 7TH

RAMONA SENTINEL

MEMBER OF THE SOUTHERN CALIFORNIA EDITORIAL ASSOCIATION

| VOL. XXVII No. 25 | RAMONA, SAN DIEGO COUNTY CAL., FRIDAY, NOVEMBER 6, 1914 | $1.50 PER YEAR |

WOMEN TAKE ACTIVE PART

Woman's Club Members Discuss Proposed Constitutional Amendments

The Ramona Woman's Club met on the 29th of October at the home of Mrs. D. O. Janeway and was promptly called to order by the president. Twenty members and four visitors were present. Roll-call was responded to by an item of joke referring to Hallowe'en.

In answer to a request by the chair a committee reports. Mrs. Dye, chairman of the "California Day" entertainment, reported a very successful meeting. It is the wish of the club to extend sincere thanks to Mrs. D. O. Janeway for her untiring efforts to make the affair a success, and to Mr. Brumhild for his help, and courtesy in conducting the meeting, etc.

The Club committee appointed to co-operate with the Farm Bureau committee—Mrs. Farm chairman—reported per Mrs. Doig) that she would attend the cleaning up of streets adjoining the High school, and asked for volunteers for other parts of town. The club resolved itself into a committee if the whole, and agreed to make Saturday a general clean-up day.

A committee was appointed by the president to secure and fit up a room to be used as a rest-room by the women and children on Back Country day.

It is learned from a later report that the committee—Mrs. Wright, Mrs. Sears, and Mrs. Ethel Johnson—has secured the brick primary building on the Grammar school grounds and will fit up.

Supervisor Porter reported through Mrs. Biles of the Improvement Club, had at this time that it was impossible to secure a fix the street near the High school, but would make temporary repairs.

New members voted into the Club were Mesdames Percy Johnson, Lillian Morris, Maude Brower, Joseph de Brown, and Miss Margaret Brown. This increases the membership to forty-three.

Mrs. Lida Wright conducted the regular program. Her paper on the origin and history of Hallowe'en, the amusements etc, was very interesting; she introduced an amusing little "ball" fortune-telling game. Instead of giving "Current Events," Mrs. Dye read a discussion on the Amendments to be voted on, as of more vital interest to the Club. Mrs. Dye had studied the subject and gave brief explanations of the questions. It was regretted that lateness of the hour precluded the study of the whole list.

The parliamentary drill was also omitted for lack of time.

The Club adjourned to meet on Nov. 12 at the home of Mrs. Sanford, Mussey's Grove.

IMPORTANT NOTICE

All persons who promised to give eatables for the big dinner on November 7th, and all others who wish to give anything in this line, please bring to the Grammar school grounds as early as possible, on Nov. 7th, where it will be taken in charge by the committee. At 12 o'clock dinner will be served to every one promptly.

MRS. H. A. MILES,
Chairman of Dinner Com.

Hallowe'en Party

Miss Ida May Roquier entertained a few friends at a Hallowe'en party Saturday evening at Ramona Hotel.

The guests were met and ushered into a room lighted by Jack-o-lanterns with weird faces which glared at one, and reminded you of spooks and things. Much fun was had in the usual games, and at a late hour, lovely refreshments were served in the dining room. The place cards were black cats. Then the guests bid the little hostess good night, and thanking her for the jolly good time.
A GUEST.

JULIAN BRINGS FAME TO SOUTHERN CALIF.
SAN DIEGO CO. EXHIBIT WINS MANY PRIZES

APPLE GROWERS ACHIEVE SUCCESS IN MAGNIFICENT EXHIBIT

Mr. Arthur Juch, Pioneer Apple Grower Tells of Victory Won in Big State Apple Show at San Francisco. Many Local Orchards Win Prizes for County and Fame for Their Owners—Julian Steadily but Surely Becoming Renowned for Its Excellent Apples. Friends Show Appreciation of Juch's Work

Our readers will be interested in the story and cut which, through the courtesy of the Union, we are able to publish this week relative to the success of Julian at the recent State Apple Show.

A reception in honor of Arthur E. Juch was given by the Foresters' Lodge, the Julian Farm Bureau and the Julian Apple Growers Association last Saturday evening in the Foresters' Hall in Julian. The organization wished in this way to express their appreciation of the work done for this section by Juch at the recent State Apple Show in San Francisco. He worked faithfully to show the section to the best advantage and succeeded in capturing thirty-three first prizes on the fruit furnished by the ranches of this section. Juch was presented with a Morris chair during the evening. In selecting refreshments for the occasion the ladies very appropriately gave first place to the apple cider made in Walter's factory at Ideal ranch.

In an interview Juch said:

"More than 250,000 people attended the Apple Show, and I found the San Francisco people are of the finest class of people that are found anywhere. The principal judge, George E. Keene, of Grand Rapids, Mich., was absolutely fair in his decisions. He was so well pleased with our fruit that he took two boxes home with him to show people that San Diego county can produce as good apples as can be grown anywhere in the world.

"I spent all my time for several weeks previous to opening of show in getting our exhibit ready. I wanted to see that all growers had an equal chance. I exhibited none of my own apples. I was prevented from making a diabolic display for the largest premium, as the time was too early in the season to obtain twenty-six boxes of one variety for my entry. I entered in five-box, one-box and plate entries.

"For our feature display I represented..."

(Continued on Page Eighth.)

FARMERS SHOULD ATTEND MEETING

Questions of Vital Interest to Back Country Farmers to be Discussed November 7th.

Editor Ramona Sentinel:
Dear Sir:

I sincerely hope that every member of every farm bureau in San Diego county will make it his specific business to attend the gathering at Ramona November 7th. It is a good deal like a business man attending his convention. He hesitates and only at the last minute does he really make up his mind to attend. Invariably when he returns home he says he would not have missed it for anything, because of the ideas he picked up.

Farming is a business; more than that, it is a science, and if any one rancher bids himself up like a snail, says he has nothing to learn and can gain nothing, and remains at home, he is making a great mistake, barring his own interests. As a rule it is the manufacturer or business man who has to be fairly dragged to a convention, who gets the most benefit out of it. Fact. Because he needs it more than anybody else. Conventions are great educators. I have seen a vast change over his entire manufacturing plant for the better, changing failure to success, because of what he "picked up" at a convention he did not think worth attending.

But this harmonious getting together of the farm bureau members means other things than the broad education of its members. One man in a community, by himself cannot accomplish a great deal. He may start things, but by himself he is helpless. For behind that man's idea of betterment or reform 500 or 1000 men thinking so he does and there is a power that railroads, common councils, legislators and others pay some attention to.

In numbers and unity there is incalculable strength. Every rancher in San Diego county should be a member of a local farm bureau and every farm bureau should keep in harmonious co-operative touch with the other bureaus. At these monthly conventions good could be accomplished beyond compare. Farming is a business, and plain and out the real-live business man who is not a member of an association and who does not back upon the value of his connection! They are the greatest educational exchanges known today.

Personally I hope that every rancher may attend at Ramona, even if he must do as did Israel Putnam, exhibit his bureau and leave his plow standing in the furrow.

Some vital questions will come up; the brush burning, run off problem, etc., and members will have an opportunity of putting themselves on record, pro or con. If, as some ranchers contend, that the heavy blanket of leaf mulch just holds the rain for the dry east winds to drink up and thus prevent a run off of the water into valleys and reservoirs, the quicker we change such a condition the better. Water Southern California must have, whether it falls from the clouds as rain or comes from the melting snows upon the mountains via the irrigating flume and ditch.

The writer hopes to be present, and may have few words to say. He wishes that every rancher in San Diego county will be there.

Respectfully,
Charles Crittenden.

Pt. Loma, California,
Oct. 28, 1914.

High School Teachers Entertain.

Misses Moffatt, Reed and McHenry entertained the pupils of the R. D. H. S. at a Hallowe'en party last Saturday evening.

All gathered at the High school and from there adjourned to the physical field near Judge Kelly's, where a bright camp fire was soon burning and a tempting roast in progress. Stories and games appropriate to the occasion were participated in and all voted their entertainers royal entertainers.

APPLE AWARD W.L. Detrick helped put Julian on the map winning this first place award for his Pine Hills apples at the 1904 St. Louis Worlds Fair. Again in 1907, Detrick came up first by winning the prestigious Wilson Medal for the best apples in the U.S. and Canada at the National Pamological Society's annual exhibition in Norfolk, Virginia.

ARTHUR JUCH, considered to be Julian's premier apple pioneer, was featured in this front page story in the November 6, 1914 edition of the Ramona Sentinel. Juch served as Julian's "apple ambassador" during the early 1900s at many fairs around the country.

ahead of his time in the development of new varieties and in promotion of Julian fruit," said Bud recently, adding, *"Among other things, Juch developed the Julian Duchess variety."*

Varieties of apples mentioned in 1880-90s newspaper stories about Julian include Bellflowers, Greenings, Baldwins, Bush's Seedlings and Duchess of Oldenburg. As one reporter put it, *"In form, size, color, flavor and quality of pulp, nothing better could be desired."*

Julian apples received top awards at the Los Angeles County fair for 22 years running. Such awards encouraged the planting of more trees.

Concern for the health of Julian orchards was expressed in a December 12, 1885 San Diego Union article: *"It is hoped no one in this county will be so foolish to risk his orchard and his neighbor's by buying trees from any but the nurseries of this county. The fact that good trees can be bought as cheap at home as anywhere while there is no risk of getting new insects into our orchards to ruin them or make them so expensive to handle that it will take all the profit to fight insects."*

More notes from the San Diego Union include one dated September 3, 1890, *"Over 100 boxes of Duchess of Oldenburg apples came down yesterday from Harry Morris' ranch near Julian for Knapp Brothers. No finer apples have been received this season."* And another item from the November 11, 1890 edition; *"Mrs. Reed drove down from her well cultivated ranch on the Julian ridge with a wagon load of Spencer Valley apples - some of the finest. The heavy fruit crop has kept them so busy that the grapes were allowed to dry on the vines."*

It wasn't too many years ago that Julian growers made their living trucking their apples out of the area to other markets. Today, however, with the tremendous number of visitors and tourists coming in, they find it necessary to import some apples in order to satisfy local demand. These are brought in from Watsonville and Guerneville, California where the quality and flavor of the fruit is very similar to Julian's.

Unfortunately, the number of acres in production has been on the decline in more recent years. According to Bud Farmer, *"there were about 500 acres producing locally in 1980 - that number is more like 300 to 400 acres today. Wholesale buyers today are more interested in how fruit looks than how it tastes. While Julian apples have the best sugar content and texture, they aren't considered pretty. People in the supermarkets buy with their eyes,"* adds Farmer.

Literally dozens of varieties are grown in Julian including some considered antique types which are found only in 60 to 80 year old orchards. The most prevalent varieties currently grown, however, are Red Delicious, Golden Delicious, Jonathan, Rome Beauty and Winesap.

While the apple may be king of Julian agriculture, it is by no means the only crop that has been grown with success in the area.

JULIAN PEARS

Some people say that Julian's pears are better than their apples, so if you like pears give them a try. Pears ripen before apples and are more available in late summer and early fall. Varieties that do well here are Bartlett, Red Bartlett, de'Anjou, Bosc and du Comice.

"For many years, from about 1925 until about 1960, there were a lot more pears than apples raised in the Julian area." according to Woody Barnes, of the Manzaita Ranch. *"In the earlier years the pears were all packed and shipped out for sale in stores. In the later years they largely went to canneries, and towards the end, the cannery was in*

PEARS WERE BIG in Julian, in fact so much so, their production out-stripped apples there from about 1925 into the 1960s. Shown here are two box labels featuring the fruit from Ray Redding's "R Ranch" and the Barnes family's "Manzanita Ranch".

Mexico. In the past, the Bartlett was the major variety produced, but presently its the de'Anjou because it has a longer season. Also, the pear is a difficult thing to handle, its good one day and bad the next where an apple has a longer shelf-life."

The following note about the fertility of the area's soil was written by Julian booster and editor James Jasper and appeared in the May 30, 1890 edition of the Julian Sentinel. We'd like to presume his little antidote is as true today, 100 years later, as it was then:

"Old friend Dan Price who lives out at the foot of Volcan Mountain, and noted for the large amount of fine berries and vegetables - was in town Saturday and as usual, brought something to gladden the hearts, tickle the palates and unloosen the purse strings of our people. They were strawberries - none of your pale, insipid, consumptive-looking berries of the coast, but real mountain berries, raised without irrigation on land so rich that to work it requires one to trim his toe-nails every night to save the toes of his boots."

APPLE DAYS

In earlier days, the community of Julian celebrated the apple with one big event, Apple Day. This was held during the month of October each year from 1949 to 1973, (with the exception of 1951 and 1964). Much credit went to Fred Grand, town booster and Chamber of Commerce president in 1949 for establishing the annual celebration. Huge crowds would drive up for that special day each year. But it got so in the final years that traffic congestion and the fall fire hazard, compounded by water shortages, convinced the town fathers it wasn't worth all the work and worry to entertain upwards of 20,000 people. They decided to stop it, but instead, to

FIRST APPLE DAY COMMITTEE, October 1909. Top, left to right, Arthur Juch, Joseph Marks and Horace Wilcox. Bottom, C.R. Wellington, F.A. DeLuca and F.L. Blanc.

put on a series of events spread-out at differnt times of the year to welcome visitors.

Starting with the annual Wild Flower show in the weeks before Mother's Day, there follows the American Legion pit barbecue on the fourth of July, the Weed Show in August, the Lions' Club Banjo and Fiddle contest in September and the Triangle Club Melodrama in October.

Actually, the first Apple Day celebration was held October 9, 1909, but didn't develop into an annual affair until some 40 years later. It was a grand event with folks invited from all over the state and attendance was

APPLE DISPLAY in Julian Town Hall, October 1909.

estimated from 200 to 2,000 (a wide ranging guess even by loose media standards).

Colorful displays of various varieties of apples was capped with a big party including an all night dance and free banquet at midnight. Even four gas buggies made it up the grade to provide a big highlight for the event. Unfortunately, there was one uninvited guest that made a mess of the affair. A full force wind blew in from the east, kicking up dust from the streets and blowing over display tents, signs and outhouses. Some of the old timers claimed it was one of the worst blows to hit Julian that they could remember. Despite the wind, the event went down in most everyone's memory as great fun anyway.

14
Schools

When the census taker had finished his job climbing hills and weaving through tents, lean-tos and the few rustic cabins that made up Julian City in July 1870, he had counted 71 children of school age. In those days 5 through 15 year olds constituted school age children.

Of the town's population of 574, there were 144 in the census that were under the age of 21, or 25% of the mining camp's total. The men who were attracted by the gold rush were a fairly representative cross section of America. Most were single, but many brought their families with them. And the kids needed to be educated.

Julian City's first school was opened in 1870 shortly after the new Board of Trustees hired its first teacher, Miss Sue E. Storms. Mike Julian was the first Clerk of the Board and served until he moved to San Diego to devote more of his time to the elected position of County Assessor. He was replaced the following year by Robert Leslie.

Miss Storms' class that first year consisted of 65

children, 29 boys and 36 girls. They met in a one room
school house 25 feet wide by 40 feet long. It was built
with green lumber. When the boards dried, they shrunk
and the knots fell out making the classroom very cold
and drafty on blustery days.

A teacher's average job tenure in Julian in those first
few years was about one year. This was due partly to the
rustic pioneer conditions and partly because most were
female. Once a teacher was engaged to be married, she
no longer taught.

By 1880, S.W. Ward was the teacher and unlike those
who preceded him, he stayed in Julian for two years. Mr.
Ward apparently adapted fairly well to the rigors of back
country tutoring. But he was not one who hesitated to
express displeasure with poor classroom conditions when
it came time each year to fill out his required report to
the County Superintendent of Schools. To the question
on the standard report form that asked *"What means of
ventilation?"* he responded in his 1881 report, *"Cracks
and absent window panes."*

Ward moved down the hill to become the first teacher
in the Santa Maria School District (Ramona) in 1882
where he continued his crusade for better school
facilities.

Milton Santee and associates purchased much of the
Santa Maria Valley in 1886 to promote a new town
named Ramona. Ward left teaching to became surveyor
for the land company, thus becoming Ramona's first
resident surveyor after having been its first teacher.

Course of study in those back country one room school
houses was sent down from the County Superintendent
of Schools. Subjects to be covered were outlined for
each grade. Basically it emphasized reading, writing and
arithmetic. The teacher taught grades one through eight
and children were promoted at the teacher's discretion.

OBERLIN DISTRICT SCHOOL- JULIAN   Photo by Elite Studio

OBERLIN DISTRICT'S one room schoolhouse was built in 1894 and located near the present corner of Farmer's and Wynola Roads.

The standard school day in those times was from nine to four, with twenty minute recesses morning and afternoon and a lunch hour.

The school day in San Diego County schools usually began with singing of a patriotic song such as *"America"*, *"Red White and Blue"* or the *"Battle Hymn of the Republic"*. Since Julian City's first school board president was also a Confederate veteran, the author rather doubts the later two songs were used in that District's earliest years. However, singing was a major part of the agenda and such old songs as *"Wait for the Wagon"*, *"Juanita"*, *"My Old Kentucky Home"* as well as other Stephen Foster tunes were class favorites.

The Julian School District has taken many forms over its near century and a quarter of existence. It was

established in 1870, being only the second district to be
organized in San Diego County. At one time, it covered
territory from Ballena to the Colorado River. This was
before creation of Imperial County.

Since 1870, twenty elementary school districts have
existed within the present day boundaries of the Julian
Union High School District. As population has shifted,
grown or declined in surrounding communities, these
districts have changed politically and/or ceased to exist.

The following is a historical summary published in the
1965 Julian Chamber of Commerce, *Apple Day Booklet.*
The booklet was published annually during the years
Julian was still celebrating Apple Days. Wallace
MacFarland had a big hand in the writing of those many
issues. This school summary was prepared by Ray
Redding, who served with distinction as Julian's high
school superintendent from 1935 to 1964:

JULIAN, 1870, became Julian Union in 1921,
   consolidating at that time with Oberlin and Orinoco.
BALLENA, 1870, was annexed to Ramona Union High
   School District in 1928.
BANNER, 1872, became part of Julian Union School
   District in 1941.
CUYAMACA, 1872, was re-formed in 1890, lapsed in
   1894, again re-formed in 1897, and annexed to Banner
   District in 1921.
OAK GROVE, 1875, became part of Warner Union
   District in 1935.
SPENCER VALLEY, 1876, is still operating in Wynola
as a one school district. This unique school functions not
only as an elementary school today but an historical
showcase for the community as well.
MESA GRANDE, 1880, became part of Julian Union
   District in 1955.

SPRING HILL, 1886, annexed to Ramona Union High School District in 1928.

ANAHUAC, 1887, in Boulder Creek below Pine Hills, near the Inaja Indian Reservation, became part of the Julian Union District in 1947.

SANTA YSABEL, 1888, at Witch Creek, became part of Julian Union District in 1955.

WARNER SPRINGS, 1888, became Warner Union in 1935, unionizing with Oak Grove and San Felipe. Operated Volcan Indian School from 1936 until discontinued in 1941.

ORINOCO, 1890, in vicinity of Pine Hills, unionized with Julian Union in 1921.

ROSEBURG, 1890, annexed to Ballena in 1904

BLOOMDALE, 1892, east of Mesa Grande, became part of Mesa Grande District in 1904.

OBERLIN, 1894, about three miles NE of Julian near Farmer's corner on Wynola Road, where the sawmill is now (1965) located, consolidated with Julian Union in 1921.

HELM, 1896, changed its name to San Felipe in 1901, Site changed from Byerles to Montezuma Valley in 1931, and unionized with Warner Springs in 1935.

PICACHO, 1901, formed from portions of Julian and Banner, transferred to Imperial County in 1907.

CHIHUAHUA, 1919, annexed to Oak Grove 1921, which became part of Warner Union in 1935.

BOREGO VALLEY, 1926, changed its name to Dry Lake in 1932, lapsed in 1937 and annexed to Borego.

BOREGO, 1931, name and spelling changed to Borrego Springs in 1950, became a unified district in 1963.

CUYAMACA UNION HIGH SCHOOL DISTRICT, was organized in 1891, opened for business in 1892, changed name to Julian Union High School in 1918.

BANNER SCHOOLHOUSE near the mouth of the San Felipe Canyon was
washed away in the flood of 1916. Volcan Mountain is in the background.

For the most part, each of the above listed districts
operating in the late nineteenth century consisted merely
of a one room schoolhouse. In those horse and buggy
days, whenever there were seven or more children, five
years of age or older without a grammar school within
walking distance, a school district could be established.
Under the County Rural School System, a school house
could be built and a teacher hired at the expense of the
local taxpayers.

In 1892, when Cuyamaca Union High School enrolled
its first pupils, there were 10 one-teacher, elementary

JULIAN HIGH SCHOOL BUS picking up students in Santa Ysabel.
Jack Bailey at the wheel.

schools in operation. In Anahuac the teacher was C.M.
Drake; in Banner, W. B. Ferguson; Helm, C. Thaw;
Julian, W. J. McLean; in Mesa Grande, L. A. Minnis;
in Orinoco, Blanch M. Boring; in Santa Ysabel, R. B.
Alderson; in Spencer Valley, Allen Peck; Spring Hill, G.
R. Ritchie and in Warner, Philip McAnany.

With one exception, all of these teachers were men,
and the majority were itinerant teachers. George Ritchie
taught for many years in the area, settled in Spencer
Valley, raised a family and ultimately became a trustee
of the High School District.

Cuyamaca Union High School District was organized
in 1891 and was the second high school district in San
Diego County. It opened its doors to the first class of

JULIAN HIGH SCHOOL ORCHESTRA photo from the 1932 year book which was organized and edited by Fred Grand. Annual featured glossy photos on everyother page. The editor also played trombone, second from right.

eleven students in 1892. Its first principal was Walter J. McLean and its first school building was located on upper Washington Street in a two-room frame house.

Although the high school enrolled its first students in 1892, it was not until 1897 that the first graduation exercises were held with four graduates receiving diplomas.

In 1912-13 J.H. Garrison was principal of the high school and decided to do something about the high incidence of cigarette smoking among students. Seems every boy in school was smoking. Garrison formed an Anti-Nicotine Club and was successful in getting the boys to stop for four months. Unfortunately, their parents were all smokers and many poked fun at the

SPENCER VALLEY school district is one of the last one-school districts in the county. Top picture as it appears today, bottom shows 1880s school.

boys. The principal found he was fighting a losing battle. Only one boy kept his pledge and stopped for good.

In 1963, ten percent of the graduating class entered Stanford University on scholarships. *"Probably no other high school in the nation could make that claim as to percentage of entry to one of the most selective schools in the country."* recalled Ray Redding proudly, but added, *"Of course, there were only 20 in our graduating class, but 10% did go to Stanford."*

Today there are 250 students enrolled in Julian High School. The school serves the largest geographical area in San Diego County. Three elementary school districts Julian Elementary, Spencer Valley and Warner Union Elementary feed students to Julian High.

15
Later Years

Over the years, mail has gotten to Julian one way or another. It started by the grace of travellers occasionally bringing it up to the mines and progressed to regular service by pony express, stage coach and motor stage. Once it was even dropped by parachute.

Julian, like most US communities, has benefitted from fast transcontinental air mail service for many years. It is relayed from San Diego to Julian by surface vehicles daily. But for one brief moment, the town's postmistress actually got her airmail directly from a low flying aircraft.

It happened on May 20, 1938 as part of a National Airmail Week celebration. A US Coast Guard plane enroute from San Diego to Phoenix dropped the mail cachet by parachute on a large canvas placed in an open field by postmistress Mrs. Edythe McGowan. By special permission from her superiors, she put a "backstamp" with a Julian postmark on the souvenir letters and had them trucked back to San Diego.

This system of direct airmail apparently didn't prove to be efficient. There is no record of its being tried in Julian again.

BACKCOUNTRY TELEPHONES

Julian City and Cuyamaca Country have tried to keep up-to-date with their communication systems for over one hundred years. The Watermans brought in the first telephone line from San Diego in 1890 to serve their Stonewall Mine and Cuyamaca City. Soon after that, Julian hooked up to it.

The 1967 *Julian Apple Day* booklet presented an interesting chronicle of early telephone service in the area. Ed Davis, Wallace Macfarlane and Margaret Surber wrote the history, and we quote: *"In 1900 Julian and Banner were connected to the line (Stonewall). The first office was in the post office at the corner of Main and B Streets and was operated by Minnie Bailey in 1902."* After being moved several times, the telephone exchange office settled into the Forester building in 1916. *"At this time there there was no night service. People living out of town, were connected to someone in town, in case of emergency, and a couple of homes were connected to long distance.*

"In 1925 Mrs. Annie Price McCreary (sister of Alice Price) became the agent for the telephone company, and she held this position until 1949 when it became dial. This meant she was paid so much to run the office, and she hired operators and paid expenses herself. Mr. and Mrs. Joe McGowan lived in the apartment in back of the office, and their daughter Minnie (Woodard) and Mildred Gray were operators. They were often called on at night in emergencies. In 1929 Arthur Price became night operator.

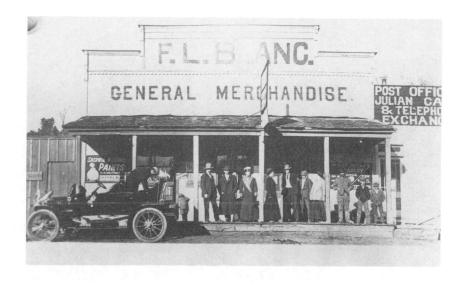

F.L. BLANC'S GENERAL STORE circa 1913. As we can see by the sign, it was next door to Julian's communications center, housing both the post office and telephone exchange. Standing in front is a Stanley Steamer automobile which was used as a small stage between Julian and San Diego.

There was a bed in the back room and he could sleep until a number dropped and a buzzer went off. He was paid fifty cents a night.

"The office was a friendly place and people would drop in to talk and hear the latest news. The operator often called people off the street if they were wanted on the phone. Radios were new and very few places had electricity. There was a radio in the office and people would call in and ask for their favorite programs. Sometimes quite a few lines would be listening until there was a call and they would have to be cut off. It seemed that nearly every girl who grew up in Julian operated the switchboard at some time.

HORSEBACK QUADRILLERS from Mesa Grande and Julian are pictured here across the street from the Robinson Hotel in 1915. Shortly after this shot was take, the hotel changed hands and was renamed the Julian Hotel.

"There was a crank on the switchboard. To get a number, you pushed a button with one hand while you cranked with the other. The operators were delighted when an electric ringer was installed, and all they had to do was press a button.

"In 1949 the office became dial and the switchboard was removed."

JULIAN'S FIRST-CLASS JAIL was designed by a professional architectural firm, Quayle Bros. & Cessy Architects. It was the only building in Julian, when it was built in 1914, to have indoor plumbing. The two cell concrete structure came in use about the time the automobile was really catching on. Since it was the constable's wife who had to feed and care for the inmates, and most of them were drunks, more and more were driven down the hill to San Diego. The jail didn't get much use.

WATER AND SEWER

In 1947, several of Julian's civic leaders decided that something had to be done about a safe and reliable source of domestic water for the entire community. Households were depending upon individual wells, and those wells in many cases were being contaminated by septic tanks and cesspools. Milo Porter, Clayton Tozer, Fred Grand, Art Blanc, Z.Y. Coleman and Ted Plueger

MAIN STREET JULIAN CAL. ON A BUSY DAY

1940s POSTCARD. Druggist Clayton Tozer made up these postcards and sold them in his store during the 1940s. He was not only poking fun at the lack of activity on Julian's Main Street then, but jabbing his friend Tom Strict for allowing his dairy cows to wander about unsupervised.

got together and formed the Julian Mutual Water Company.

"With the help of Milo Porter," said Fred Grand, who was president of that company, *" we borrowed enough money to put in a reservoir and water system in town. We got our water from springs on Volcan Mountain and through Mrs. Ayres of Whispering Pines."*

When the Julian Community Services District was formed, it took over the operation, maintenance and expansion of Julian's water system.

SLUSHY STREET SCENE at the corner of Washington and Main taken in 1932, before Julian got Main Street paved.

In times of prolonged drought Julian suffers from water shortages just like the rest of San Diego County communities. But in December 1990 the town suffered a dry spell that couldn't be blamed on a drought. Below-freezing temperatures shortly before Christmas burst customer's water lines in more than sixty places. Within forty-eight hours the District's entire 366,000 gallons of storage capacity drained away down town gutters. With loss of water pressure, the hydraulically operated pumps failed. In order to restore pressure to get the system operating again, the District had to truck in water from Ramona. Since then the District has installed manual backup for the pumps.

Julian's first sewer system was installed by the Federal Works Project Administration in 1936, but it only served a couple of blocks in downtown.

The Julian Sanitation District, a County agency, was formed in November 1945. In 1953, several thousand feet of sewer line were installed throughout the old townsite and a large septic tank type of treatment plant constructed. By 1962, there was 7,900 total feet of sewer line servicing an area of 63 acres. The treated effluent went to Franklin Barnes' apple orchard.

16

Park Trails

Monument Trail winds from the northeast corner of Green Valley Campgrounds, along Airplane Ridge and on to Japacha Peak. About one and seven tenths miles up that steep trail, a path leads off to the left to a World War I Liberty airplane engine mounted on a stone base. Set in the base is a bronze plaque to memorialize two Army officers who lost their lives on this mountain many years ago. The story goes back to a cloudy December morning in 1922.

After waiting more than an hour past scheduled departure for clouds to clear over the Cuyamacas, 1st Lt. Charles L. Webber took off at 9:15 A.M. December 7th in his de Havilland DH-4B biplane. His passenger was Col. Francis C. Marshall, assistant to the Chief of U.S. Army Cavalry on an inspection tour of cavalry garrisons around the country. They left Rockwell Field at North Island, Coronado headed for Tucson and Camp Hearn. But clouds still lingered over the mountains as the biplane started to climb east.

Bad weather always worried Major Henry "Hap" Arnold, Webber's commanding officer, and he had instructed the 26 year old lieutenant to return to Rockwell if he encountered problems getting through the clouds. Arnold later became the first and only air force officer to hold the rank of five-star general while commanding the U.S. Air Force during World War II.

Lieutenant Webber was an accomplished young flyer with over 600 hours in eight different kinds of military aircraft. He flew with Lt. James "Jimmy" Doolittle and was one who escorted him on the last leg of his record breaking one-stop, trans-continental flight of September 1922.

These were lean times for an Army Air Service which had few aircraft and was fighting for every penny it could get from Congress. While war-impoverished Great Britain was committing $350 million to enlarge and modernize its Royal Air Force, the U.S. Congress was cutting General William "Billy" Mitchell's appropriations request from $83 million to $25 million.

Major Arnold, like other aviation leaders of the day, was continually working to sell air power and attract attention to the potential benefits of flying. He also was very concerned for the men and machines of his command and didn't want to see unnecessary chances taken. Shortly after Webber took off, Arnold felt apprehensive and followed in his SE-5 pursuit plane, but was unable to overtake Webber and turned back over Chollas Heights in East San Diego.

Later that morning, another Army Air Service pilot landed at Rockwell Field having flown west from Brooks Field, San Antonio. He told Arnold he had climbed to an altitude of 10,000 feet without topping the clouds over the east San Diego County mountains. He and the

DH-4B de HAVILLAND BIPLANE flown by the Army Air Service in the 1920s. Pictured at Rockwell Field, later taken over by the Navy called North Island today. Webber crashed the DH-4B on Middle Peak in December 1922.

pilot of a second Army plane then descended and picked their way through mountain passes just below the clouds. A third pilot in that flight didn't like what he saw and turned his plane back to land at El Centro.

When Webber failed to report in by the following morning, an air search was launched. Days passed but no clues were found. Before the main search was finally abandoned on December 18th, 42 planes and nearly 100 Army and Navy pilots and observers were involved in an air effort that covered the deserts and mountains from San Diego to Arizona and south into Mexico. Cavalry

from Fort Huachuca, Arizona and Infantry from Camp
Stephen Little, Nogalas engaged 450 men in a ground
search.

While the main search centered in Arizona, Major
Arnold felt strongly Webber had crashed in the
mountains. Witnesses at Viejas, Descanso, Guatay and
Morena Dam had reported seeing a plane on that fateful
morning. Using a road map, Arnold traced a sequence
of sightings that suggested Webber had flown
southeastward towards Campo. Further air and ground
search of the Cuyamacas, however, failed to locate the
wreckage.

It wasn't until six months after the disappearance, May
12th, that cattleman George McCain came upon the
crash site hidden in a pocket of brush on Japacha Peak.
Personal effects found in the wreckage, and the serial
number on the engine verified it was the missing plane.
A reward had been offered for finding the plane. When
McCain "come down off that mountain, he thought he
was the richest cowboy in the whole state," recalled
Granville Martin, "but they called it off (the reward).
Why, you could've bought him for a quarter."

Arnold had maintained that Webber was too good a
pilot to stray far off course, and he was right. The
wreckage lay within a few miles of the flight plan.

On Sunday, May 23, 1923, 70 civilian employees from
Rockwell Field climbed to the crash site and erected the
monument we see today. They mixed concrete, affixed
the plaque and held a brief memorial service. A few
days later, Arnold and several fellow officers returned to
the site. They carefully removed one of the stones at the
monument's base and inserted a three foot metal tube
then carefully replaced the stone so as to leave no trace.
Sealed in the tube was a list of officers, men and
civilians at Rockwell Field, as well as three copies of the

LIBERTY ENGINE from the crash was made into this memorial by officers and workers from Rockwell Field, May 1923. The memorial still stands today.

San Diego Union that described the search. The tube has long since been removed.

Arnold later wrote to Webber's parents, "This monument lies high in the mountains in a lonely spot, difficult to reach, and will probably be seldom visited on account of these difficulties."

While he was right about the difficulty of the trail, the climb to the monument makes a pleasant hike, at the same time providing a glimpse back into those years when flying was still very much a pioneering experience.

CUYAMACA STATE PARK HISTORY

About sixty percent of Don Agustin Olvera's old
Mexican land grant, the Cuyamaca Rancho, became a
California State Park in January 1933. This constituted
most of the 26,000 acres that Governor Robert
Waterman had bought along with the Stonewall Mine in
1885.

Waterman had brought in the necessary capital and
seen the mine operate at its most productive levels. But
the cycle of boom and bust caught up with the
Stonewall. In 1892 Waterman died, and by 1893 the
accessible ore had pinched out and operations went on
the decline.

The Sather Banking Company of San Francisco
acquired the property upon Waterman's death, and
applied cyanide reduction methods of processing the
tailing. But it seemed they were fighting a losing battle.
In 1907, the very thing Waterman had feared when the
Flume Company created the Cuyamaca Lake happened.
New tunnels being dug could not be drained properly
and operations had to be stopped.

In 1917 the bank sold the property to Colonel A.G.
Gasson who held it for six years before selling it to
Ralph M. Dyar in 1923. The 21,000 acres went for
$200,000.

Dyar was a retired businessman from Detroit who had
moved west to Beverly Hills, California. He wasted no
time in setting out to make his new acquisition a
showcase mountain retreat. The stone building which
currently houses the park headquarters and Indian
museum was the first major improvement and he
referred to it as his "mountain cabin". Roads were
improved and bridges built.

LAKE CUYAMACA, looking north from the top of Stonewall Peak. In the background is North Peak, elevation 5,993'. The hike to the top is a pleasant experience and takes the average person in relatively good condition little less than an hour. Shown here is Glen Young and his Grandpa.

By 1933, the great depression had settled in, and also according to Hero Rensch, " the Dyars finally tired of their plaything." Dyar offered the State of California the property for public park use for half its appraised value. The State took him up on it and the public has been the beneficiary ever since.

At the beginning, no campgrounds or other recreational facilities existed and few trails were improved for hiking. The depression had spawned the CCC (Civilian Conservation Corps), and they went to work getting the new park in shape for public use. Harvey W. Moore had been Dyar's ranch foreman and he became the park's first supervisor. Much of the basic improvements which made the parkusable for the public were put in during those early days.

March 1940, saw the opening of the first organizational camp facility within the park boundary. The San Diego County Boy Scout Council negotiated a lease for Camp Haul-cu-cuish which has been enjoyed by three generations of scouts and is still operating today.

TRAILS

Today the park has well over a hundred miles of riding and hiking trails. The popular 3.5 mile *CUYAMACA PEAK TRAIL,* which is moderately difficult, climbs to the summit for a spectacular view of the ocean, the desert, Mexico, and the Salton Sea.

STONEWALL PEAK overlooks Cuyamaca Lake and the old mine. It's a two mile hike to the top that climbs from 4,800 to 5,700 feet elevation. There are many switchbacks which help keep the hike at the moderate level of difficulty.

The difficult 9 mile *HARVEY MOORE TRAIL* begins near the Sweetwater River Bridge half a mile north of Green Valley. It goes to the scenic East Mesa, passing the Granite Spring Trail Camp and continues through Harper Creek Canyon. The average hiker should allow eight hours for this one.

PASO SELF-GUIDED NATURE TRAIL is short and easy and will introduce the hiker to native plants. It starts at the Paso Picacho picnic grounds.

toward funeral expenses to those who qualify. The National Funeral Directors Association states the typical cost of an adult funeral is between $5,000 and $10,000. **YOUR FAMILY WILL BE RESPONSIBLE FOR THE UNPAID BALANCE!**

GET THE FACTS! Return the card below in the enclosed postage paid envelope today to receive information about a final expense life insurance program that can pay up to $25,000 to your beneficiary. This plan is designed to prevent a financial burden on your survivors. You may qualify for full coverage immediately even with a health condition.

I look forward to hearing from you soon.

Sincerely,

James Canoy

James A Canoy

PS: THIS IS A RESPONSIBILITY YOU SHOULD NOT IGNORE!

4LSML-R

ACHTUNG!! - ACHTUNG!! - ACHTUNG!!

WARNUNG!!

DIESES GEBEIT WIRD VON VIEL

WACHT PUSSYKOTZEN BEWACHT!!

ACHTUNG!! - WARNUNG!! - ACHTUNG!!

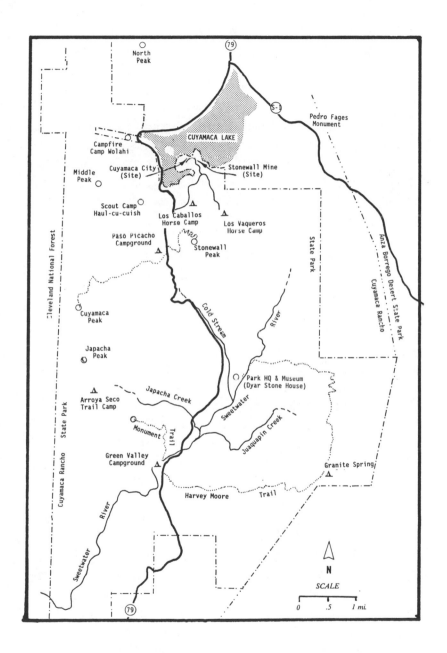

CUYAMACA RANCHO STATE PARK

The State Park offers a variety of camping facilities, for both man and beast. Family campsites are available at both Paso Picacho and Green Valley, while the former campground also offers sites for groups of up to 60 people.

Two equestrian campsites are located just south of Cuyamaca Lake. They are *Los Caballos Campground* and *Los Vaqueros Campground.* The former accommodates family riders, and is complete with campsites for people and corrals for the horses. The latter also is equipped to handle equestrian groups of up to 80 people and 45 horses.

Primitive trail camps are located at *Arroyo Seco and Granite Springs.* Each is greatly limited as to the number of people they can handle.

HEISE PARK

The State Park isn't the only place for interesting hiking, camping and beautiful views. The County of San Diego operates William Heise Park located on the western slope of Cuyamaca's North Peak.

William H. Heise was an inventor and farmer who wanted to see his land used for the enjoyment of the public. In 1967 he offered to give the County 131 acres free of charge. He later revised the offer to a total of 211 acres for $68,072 if the County would develop and open a public park right away. The county took him up on the deal and the park was dedicated in 1970.

It is reached by turning onto the Pine Hills Road from Highway 78. Visitors to Pine Hills Lodge and the bed and breakfast inns in the area consider this park not only convenient, but one of their favorite places to hike.

In addition to hiking and picnicing, the park offers a limited number of tent and motorhome camping sites.

17

Conservation and Preservation

When Judge Benjamin Hayes visited the site of the ancient Indian Village of Yguai (Iguai) in July 1870, he was struck by the beauty of the setting. The village, which had been a prehistoric center of trade and culture in the Cuyamacas, was situated just a few hundred yards northeast of the present 'Y' intersection of State Highway 79 and County S-1, the Sunrise Highway.

The most striking feature of the landscape, Hayes noted, was, *"the trees around this rancheria bearing both large and small acorns, are very thick, up to the top of the Peak - so that one can scarcely find his way out the same as he may go into the forest, can only see the sky above him."*

Two years later, naturalist James Cooper journeyed through the same area and was similarly awed by the scene. *"The road now going northward led us over the east base of the northern peak, where I was much surprised at passing through one of the densest forests I have seen in California, for a distance of about five miles, consisting of*

two (species) live oaks and sugar pine, the former
sometime five to seven feet in diameter."

Today, the scene bears no resemblance to that
described by Hayes or Cooper over 120 years ago. Since
then, much of that land has been denuded for its timber
and fire wood.

The Stonewall Mine was located a short distance from
this area. The mine not only extracted a considerable
amount of gold ($2 million worth at $20.67per oz.)
during the 1880s and 90s but, in so doing, consumed a
tremendous amount of forest.

Timbers were needed for tunnels and fire wood for
boilers. During the mine's bonanza days it ran twenty-
four hours a day on two twelve hour shifts. It took three
firemen to feed the boilers which drove the pumps, the
hoist and the stamp mill. Thirty cords of wood were
consumed every day. At one time a crew of 40   Russians
were imported from Baja California to cut the oak at
two dollars per cord.

Add to that the oak wood consumed for fuel by settlers
in the area, and we can see why it didn't take much time
to denude the lush forest of the valley and lower slopes
of North Peak.

There would have been more cutting and loss of
Cuyamaca forest land, had not a few far-sighted
individuals decided to do something about it in the early
twentieth century.

In 1910, Colonel Ed Fletcher learned that the owner of
extensive woodlands, ranging from Boulder Creek to
Pine Hills, planned to build a saw mill and log off the
trees. With an eye primarily to saving the forest, but
another toward developing remote homesites, Fletcher
persuaded San Diego merchant George Marston and
banker M. T. Gilmore to join him in buying out the
owner.

A subdivision map for Pine Hills was recorded in 1912. Resulting parcels and lots were sold with deed restrictions designed to save the trees. No living trees could be cut except for roadways and homes without permission of the U.S. forest service.

VOLCAN MOUNTAIN

Volcan Mountain stands today as another example of sensitive conservation practices during this century. While most San Diego County mountains have been logged to some extent since the arrival of the Spanish two centuries ago, Volcan was the last to see large-scale commercial logging. As one of the largest distinctive land masses in the County, it extends in a northwest direction from Banner Grade to the Santa Ysabel Valley.

The Grand family sunk their roots into Volcan Mountain shortly after August Grand Sr. immigrated from France in 1871. He homesteaded Arkansas Canyon, above San Felipe Valley, and much of Volcan Mountain and raised cattle.

In more recent years, Fred A. Grand, third generation to own the land, was one of three loggers who harvested about 20 million board feet of lumber from the mountain between 1945 and 1956. Hugh Crumpler, noted feature writer for the San Diego Union, took a trip up Volcan with Grand and the author shortly before Fred died in 1990. He wrote about the conservation methods practiced by those last loggers on Volcan.

Today, pine, ceder, spruce and fir stand tall above rotting stumps that are the only clues of earlier commercial logging. Recalling the practices of those last loggers on Volcan, Grand was quoted, *"Look around this mountain and you'll be hard-pressed to find two stumps that aren't separated by several mature trees. Fact is, until you get into the forest- under the trees - you might not know that any logging had gone on at all."* said Grand.

"When I started logging in 1945, I had two-man teams of lumberjacks'" he added, *"It took a team half an hour to fell a 30-inch tree with a 6-foot crosscut saw - one man on each end of the saw and on opposite sides of the tree. Along came the chain saw and it took two or three minutes."*

Grand operated a saw mill and planing mill on Volcan, and at one point in time had as many as 40 lumberjacks cutting trees for lumber and poles.

The scene today in Pine Hills and Volcan is a tribute to some of those earlier San Diego County businessman-conservationists who appreciated the need for protecting our forestlands while providing needed homes and forest products for humans as well.

Volcan Mountain with its beautiful stands of incense ceder, Coulter pine, big cone spruce and white fir is the fountainhead of two of San Diego County's primary waterways, the San Dieguito and the San Diego River basins.

The San Dieguito River winds from its Volcan origin some 55 miles to Del Mar before it ends its journey to the sea. Ironside Spring, tucked into Volcan's west side at the 4,600 foot elevation, is the fountainhead. It has been pumping pure water at the rate of about fifteen gallons a minute, day in and day out since man can remember. Whoever named it Ironside, is not known for sure. But its been on the maps as such for many years.

As the water rolls west, and is joined by many other springs and streams, its course becomes associated with several valleys named for saints, and is named for two -

IRONSIDE SPRINGS
is the fountainhead of
the San Dieguito River
basin. Pictured here in
1990 next to the springs
is former Volcan Mountain
landowner and timberman
Fred Grand.

Santa Ysabel Creek, San Pasqual, San Bernardo and San Dieguito River.

This association led Col. Ed Fletcher to suggest back in the 1920s that it be called the "All Saints River".

Volcan's other offspring, the San Diego River, has its head waters beginning about two miles northwest of Wynola Valley on the mountain's lower south slope.

But the major flows that account for the San Diego River's early identity are generated by the Cuyamaca Mountains. Such creeks as the Boulder and Conejo make up much of the flow that is captured by the El Capitan Dam. Maybe that's the reason Volcan doesn't get much credit for fathering the river that has played such a prominent role in San Diego history.

In recent years two organizations have been formed to convert part of this Volcan Mountain to public land and preserve it for open space and trails. One is a public agency, the San Dieguito River Park Authority and the other, Volcan Mountain Preserve Foundation.

The former's plans call for creation of a San Dieguito River Valley Park. This involves the ultimate acquisition of a 55 mile corridor containing 66,000 acres. The park would run from near the top of Volcan Mountain to the shore in Del Mar.

The latter group is private, consisting mainly of Julian area volunteers. So far they have been successful in gaining 210 acres for the preserve and are optimistic about the County acquiring another 500 acres. This would come from grant funds enabling the purchase of part of the Rutherford Family's 5,440 acre Volcan holdings.

FIRES

Periodically mother nature has a way of thinning out the dense growth that accumulates in our back country with disastrous forest fires. This seems to happen about every twenty years. It's happened twice in Cuyamaca country in this generation's memory.

In the summer of 1950 the most devastating fire in the recorded history of the Cuyamacas laid waste 64,000 acres. It started in the Canajos Creek area of the Capitan Grande Indian Reservation on August 16th. A combination of high daytime temperatures and low humidity set the stage for the disaster. Before some 1,300 firefighters could contain the flames, the strong westerly winds had spread the fire into the Cuyamaca Rancho State Park burning over half its acreage.

JULIAN'S LIBRARY originally served as a one-room school house in Witch Creek from 1888 until 1954. Seeing the possibilities of saving part of our heritage while providing a needed public facility, the Julain Historical Society moved the building to Julian, rehabilitated it and donated it to the County for a public library in 1974. Leading this drive were Ray Redding, Richard Zerbe, Charles Vilinek and Glen Wilkinson. Shown here, the project before and after.

Again in September 1970, the devastating Laguna fire roared through thousands of acres of mountainland leaving blackened forest and ash on city streets in San Diego some 40 miles away.

Mindful of the need to remove excess brush periodically, the State Parks Department, State Department of Forestry and U.S. Forest Service practice programs designed to remove dense concentrations of potential forest fire fuel.

The forestry agencies call their programs 'controlled burns'. The parks people prefer to conduct 'prescribed burns'. While techniques and nomenclature may differ somewhat, the purpose and effect are the same, man is removing excess plant material before mother nature removes more than we want.

JULIAN HISTORICAL DISTRICT

In 1978, the County of San Diego established by ordinance a Julian Historic District. This was done for the purpose of preserving and enhancing the historic character of the town. An Architectural Review Board, acting with the weight and authority of County government, reviews all building permits and must pass on an applicant's plans before construction permits are approved. In the forefront of establishing and maintaining the program has been Richard Zerbe, architect, town historian and resident of Julian for over 43 years.

Like most programs which involve government control and seemingly subjective decisions, the process becomes controversial at times. Generally speaking, however, buildings with historical value have been preserved and new construction designed which complement Julian's heritage.

18
Back Country 1992

COUNTRY CARRIAGES has been in business in Julian since 1985. Owner Suzanne Porter operates two old fashioned rigs which are outfitted to provide a comfortable, as well as interesting historical tour around Julian. Shown here is associate Wayne Morretti taking two bundled passengers for a look at the sights.

MENGHINI WINERY has been producing award-winning fine wines in Julian since 1984. Mike and Toni Menghini are shown here in their tasting room at the winery which is located at the end of Farmers Road.

THE JULIAN HAND BELLS. Besides having fun, the ringers perform around the county for different clubs and events. Formed in 1986, the group consists of 10 bell ringers and is directed by Donna Cook.

FIDDLE AND BANJO CONTEST is held each September in the Frank Lane Park by the Julian Lions Club. It attracts several thousand people each year with proceeds going to benefit the club's sight and hearing program. The 1992 event will mark the 22nd year the Julian Lions have held this popular contest.

PINE HILLS LODGE The Dinner Theater operates year round. Dave Goodman, a retired corporate marketing director, bought the lodge in 1980 and conceived the idea of a dinner theater. He produces five shows a year. Performances on Friday and Saturday and an occasional Sunday. The only time the theater is dark is between productions when they take a week or two to build new sets. The Lodge's rooms and cottages offer a rustic, warm retreat for its urban guests. It has been in continuous operation since 1912 when Colonel Ed Fletcher built it to help promote lot sales in his new Pine Hills development. It was preceded by the Pine Hills Hotel built around the turn of the century by W.L. Detrick a short distance north of the present establishment. That earlier building burned down about 1908.

The structure used as today's theater was originally built as a training gymnasium (opposite) for champion heavy-weight boxer Jack Dempsey in 1926. The owner of the lodge at that time was Fred A. Sutherland, prominent San Diego stage and Yellow Cab owner. Sutherland, a boxing fan and friend of Dempsey brought him to Pine Hills to train for his fight with Gene Tunney. Dempsey lost the match and his title but Sutherland got a lot of publicity for his lodge, never the less.

EAGLE & HIGH PEAK MINES adjoin each other under ground. Standing in front of the Eagle Mine entrance with one of its ore carts from the 1870s are Harlen Nelson, proprietor with associates Dennis P. Busgen, dog Maxwell and Karl Nelson. Mine is open for conducted tours seven days a week and appears very much as it did when it was being worked in earlier days.

100.1 FM RADIO STATION KBNN broadcasts from the new commercial center in Santa Ysabel and transmits from its tower atop 5,783' Volcan Mountain. KBNN first went on the air in October 1991 and serves the 1,200 square miles that constitutes San Diego County's heartland. Founders and owners are local residents Harold Schachter, John and Marie Singer and Andy and Karyen Smith.

THE JULIAN NEWS is the only independently owned weekly newspaper serving San Diego County back country today. Established in 1985, it has a current circulation of 3,000. Besides covering Julian and Cuyamaca it is read in communities as far south as Boulevard and Jacumba, north in Ranchita and Palomar Mountain, east in Borrego Springs and west to Ramona. Publisher and general manager is Michael Judson-Carr and Karen O'Rourke is editor.

EDUCATIONAL LEADERS in front of Julian High School in 1992 are Ray Redding, left, who served as principal and district superintendent from 1935 until 1964 with current principal Chet Francisco. Redding saw school enrollment grow from 90 when he started, to 200 in 1964. Today, there are 250 students in Julian H.S. In the background is the "Alumni Bell" that hung in the original high school 1896 until the 1940s. Julian High School District serves three elementary districts; Julian, Warner Springs and Spencer Valley.

LITTLE CHANCE OF THE TOWN HALL burning to the ground again. Today Julian has the latest in fire fighting equipment backed by a force of 35 volunteer firefighters and paramedics. Pictured in front of the fire station are two of the volunteers, Captain Ken Kremensky and Marion Reynolds, emergency medical techician.

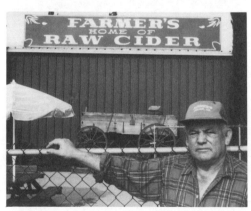

APPLE PIES AND MORE are found at the Farmer family's store in Wynola. Bud Farmer has been a Julian school trustee and life long community leader.

BED AND BREAKFAST HOMESTAY INNS are providing today the kind of old fashioned hospitality our back country hotels did a century ago. In June 1991, a dozen such Julian establishments formed an industry guild to assure quality control and easy reservation service for their mountain visitors. Pictured in front of the *Julian White House* are proprietors of seven such inns. Left to right: Mary Ellen Thilken, *Homestead B&B;* Gil Archambou, *Rockin' A Ranch;* Mary Marvin, *Julian White House B&B;* Mary Trimmins, *Butterfield Bed & Breakfast;* Carol Pike, *Mountain High B&B;* Idaleen Potter, *Villa Idaleen B&B* and Shari Helsel, *Random Oak Ranch*

APPLE PIE SPECIALISTS The Smothers family owns and operates the Julian Pie Company. They think nothing of baking and serving 1,000 apple pies on any busy weekend day. Pictured by their pie wagon are brothers, Dan, Dace and Tim with mother Liz. Patriarch Keith was back at the family ranch planting more apple trees when this picture was taken. Liz estimates that between all the apple pie purveyors, Julian bakes and sells 250,000 pies a year.

ANOTHER HO-HUM SUNDAY AFTERNOON ON MAIN STREET

NOTED SCULPTOR JIM HUBBELL has been at work in his showcase studio complex on Orchard Lane for thirty years. His works can be found throughout the country. One recent design, which he contributed to the community, is for the gateway to the new Volcan Mountain Preserve trail.

JULIAN HISTORICAL MUSEUM has been operating in its present location since 1950. It is run by the Julian Women's Club, whose president Lehla Porter (right) is pictured here with curator Mable Carlson. The building was first built to serve as a brewery in the mid-1880s by Peter Meyerhofer who operated other beer establishments in San Diego. The Julian brewery lasted about three years before the building was sold and converted to a blacksmith shop operating there until the early 1930s.

PRESERVATIONIST, architect, historian Richard Zerbe has lived in Julian for over 43 years. He was a leader in the establishment of Julian's Historic District and Architectural Review Board. Zerbe continues to champion the cause for preserving the town's historical flavor.

NOTED FOR FLOWERS as well as apples and pears, the Barnes family has
been active in Julian since the 1880s. Manzanita Ranch has been a favorite
stop for travellers to the mountains since 1907. Woody Barnes is shown here
with the lilacs which grow across the road from their store. The family was
famous for their outstanding flower displays at San Diego's Marston
Department Store from the 1940s through the 1960s.

PARK SUPERINTENDENT JACK SHU is responible for operation of the Cuyamaca Rancho State Park. Shown here with the Indian cultural exhibit located at park headquarters at the south end of Green Valley.

THE OLD AND THE NEW ON MAIN STREET. One of the few old
fashioned soda fountains in San Diego County is found in Herb & Jody
Scholick's Julian Drug Store (below). At the other end of town center are the
new Stonewall Shops sporting the modern version of an ice cream parlor.
Architecture for the center was inspired by the Stonewall Mine.

CEREMONIES celebrating acquisition of the first 210 acres for the Volcan Mountain Preserve were held in the Julian Town Hall January 1990. On stage are shown Smokey Bear with Cleveland National Forest Superintendent Dennis Orbus and associate. Local leaders in the preserve foundation include Peter Bergstrom, Francis Hemsher, Lynn Horton, Anne Hubbell and Clint Powell.

APPENDIX A

SUMMARY OF 1870 JULIAN CENSUS

A. Number of households
   (includes single bedrolls and tents). = 306
B. Total Population count   = 574
C. Number under 21 years of age   = 144 (25%)
D. School age, between 5 and 15   = 71 (12%)

E. Breakdown by occupation, trade and profession:

Gold Miner	93	Domestic Servant	3
Keeping House	80	Cabinent Maker	3
(all female)		Quartzmill Worker	3
Carpenter	38	Lawyer	2
Farm Laborer	23	Retail Grocer	2
Laborer	20	Restaurant Keeper	2
Farmer	18	Hotel Keeper	2
Trader	10	Gunsmith	2
Saloon Keeper	9	Harness Maker	2
Painter	7	Livery Stable Keeper	2
Steam Engineer	7	One each of the following:	
Butcher	6		
Blacksmith	5	Civil Engineer	
Brick/stone Mason	5	Dentist	
Teamster	4	Amalgamator	
Laundryman	4	Shoemaker	
(all Chinese)		Hatter	
Millwright	3	Lumber Dealer	
Cooper	3	Chairmaker	
Ranchman	3	Assayer	
Store Clerk	3	Druggist	
Machinist	3	Druggist Clerk	
Teacher	3	Barber	
Stock Raiser	3	Ship Sawyer	
Stone Cutter	3	Gas Filler	
Baker	3	Hearder	

APPENDIX B

The San Diego Union published a summation of the Cuyamaca grant boundary survey case in the form of a poem on December 21, 1873. The author is unknown, only referring to himself as "Semper Paratus".

Ye Stalwart sons of labor, who live within this state
An interesting history in you I will relate.
Tis of the Cuyamaca Grant, which everyone must own
To be the most gigantic feud that ever yet was known
The swindle was projected when first our mines were found -
When Pascoe made his false survey, to take in all our ground
Their scheme was not successful, although they ran their lines
To survey in our farming lands, and also take our mines.
We soon employed a lawyer this false survey to fight,
And Hardenburgh decided that we were in the right.
The case was sent to Washington and what did Drummond do
But send it back immediately to have it tried anew.
Our witnesses were ready when the case came on again,
And from the evidence adduced it seemed to us quite plain;
And everyone did testify who knew the County well
That the Rancho Cuyamaca did not join the San Ysabel
And it was further proven, both by Trimmes and by Ames,
That Ocampo herded cattle here, regardless of their claims.
And Escherich also testified that where his house did stand,
Was known and recognized by all to be on public land.
Augustin Olvera too, the grantee to the land,

Told a very curious tale, when he got on the stand.
He spoke of how he got the Ranch, and where it ought to be,
And that the Valle de las Viejas was its southern boundary.
The Diseno also was produced, on which our claims we fix;
As by that, they got their grant confirmed in eighteen fifty six.
Establishing, beyond a doubt, in all unbiased minds,
That Julian was at least two leagues north of its northern lines
Now when these knaves discovered that they were in a trap,
They called up Don Juan Warner, who swore he made the map
He proved his memory very thin, and well that title earns,
For it was proven on the stand, 'twas made by Able Stearns.
The papers went to Hardenburgh, who openly disclosed
The same opinion as before, and that he felt disposed
To tell the Land Commission that he no cause could find
To reverse his first decision, or ought to change his mind
But would send the proofs to Washington, that he might understand
Whether the mines were on the grant or on the public land.
The Commissioner decided, to his honor it be said,
That the surveys be rejected, and a new survey was made
Being guided by the Fox map along its Northern line.
And a survey made accordingly, which would the grant confine

Within its legale boundaries, for
Drummond did decree
That Cuyamaca northern peak its
northern line should be
But while the case was pending these
grant men went in haste
To swear out an induction to restrain
us from all waste.
Subpoenas then were issued and served
on every one
Of the farmers and the miners for the
mischief they had done
For the farmers had built houses to
protect them from the cold
And the miners had dug up the soil
and robbed it of its gold
Valued at ten-thousand dollars, so the
complainant swore
And if all depended on his oath would
add ten-thousand more.
He forced us to make answer, which
we sent at once above,
Unto the U.S. Circuit Court, in which
we hope to prove
That the lands, which we now occupy,
to the Government belong,
And that granting an induction would
be doing us wrong.
The induction I will cast aside and now
proceed to tell
What happened when the news arrived,
and afterwards befell.
Upon arrival of the stage the news
spread throughout the street
That the survey was rejected and that
we had beaten Treat.
We stuffed some clothing full of straw,
and round it we did flock
And marched the figure through the
streets till it was twelve o'clock.
We hung it then upon a pole, and
every person by
Could read the placard on its breast.
"John Treat, today you will die!"
Swinging on a pole all day, exposed to
public sight,

His grotesque figure seemed to fill the
boys with delight;
At night bonfires were kindled, and
people thronged the street,
To participate in the burning of the
effigy of Treat.
But Treat is not the worst of them, at
least so we've been told.
For Luco is notorious as an operator
bold.
There are some persons living here of
whom I know will speak,
Who have been at all our meetings and
around among . . .
Gleaning news for wretches who would
rob us of our homes
Disappearing and appearing to us like
so many gnomes,
To which I say, take warning, or you
will surely meet
A fate, perhaps, ten times as bad as
that of poor John Treat.
Mr. Hartman was out generaled, with
all his witty ways,
And by our able counselor, the
talented Judge Hayes
Who won our case most nobly, not
withstanding all our fears,
And to him for it, I now propose to
give three rousing cheers,
Now comes an able lawyer, one of the
mighty throng
That swell our Nation's Capital, who
helped our case along.
And labored for us faithfully without
retaining fee.
I speak of St. Clair Denver, so give him
three times three.
Now give three cheers for Julian, and
her hardy sons of toil,
For well I know each manly breast with
gratitude doth boil;
For those who helped us in our need,
let daughter and let son
Shout with their songs of gratitude,
that our case is won.

References & Resources

GENERAL REFERENCES

Several publications and manuscripts were used by the author which covered a number subjects:

Fletcher, Col. Ed, MEMOIRS, Private printing 1952, San Diego (MEMOIRS)

Jasper, James A., TRAIL-BREAKERS AND HISTORY-MAKERS, Unpublished manuscript, 1934, San Diego Historical Society Archives. (TBAHM)

Jasper, James A., JULIAN AND ROUND ABOUT, Unpublished manuscript, 1928, author's collection (JARA)

Julian Sentinel Newspaper, Microfilms, California State Library, Sacramento, (Copies from San Diego Genealogical Society)

Ramona Sentinel Newspaper, Ramona Pioneer Historical Society

San Diego, County of, Clerk of the Board of Supervisors records, and County Clerk recordings

San Diego Union, Daily and Weekly Newspaper, Microfilms, San Diego Public Library, California Room and San Diego Historical Society Archives

San Diego Daily World Newspaper, Microfilms, San Diego Public Library, California Room

Sheldon, Gale W., JULIAN GOLD MINING DAYS, Master's Thesis, San Diego State College, 1958 (JGMD)

INDIANS

Cline, Lora L., JUST BEFORE SUNSET, LC Enterprises, Tombstone, Arizona, 1984

Hayes, Benjamin, NOTES ON THE INDIANS OF SAN DIEGO COUNTY, with foreword and notes by Arthur Woodward, The Masterkey, Sept. 1934, Published by Southwest Museum, Los Angeles, Calif.

Hedges, Kenneth and Christina Beresford, SANTA YSABEL ETHNOBOTANY, San Diego Museum of Man, San Diego, 1986

Kroeber, A.L., HANDBOOK OF THE INDIANS OF CALIFORNIA, Dover Publications, Inc., New York, 1925

Johnson, Mary Elizabeth, INDIAN LEGENDS OF THE CUYAMACA MOUNTAINS, Privately printed, San Diego, 1914

Pourade, Richard F., *TIME OF THE BELLS*, Union Tribune
Publishing Co., San Diego, 1961
Rensch, Hero Eugene, *THE INDIAN PLACE NAMES OF RANCHO
CUYAMACA*, California Department of Parks and Recreation, 1950
Rensch, Hero Eugene, *FAGES' CROSSING OF THE CUYAMACAS*,
San Diego Historical Society Journal, September 1955
True, Delbert L., *INVESTIGATION OF A LATE PREHISTORIC
COMPLEX IN CUYAMACA RANCHO STATE PARK*, University
of California, Los Angeles, 1970

INDIANS - INTERVIEWS BY AUTHOR:
Foster, Danial G., *Anthropology Program Manager, California
Department of Forestry*, July 1991
Hedges, Kenneth, *Director, San Diego Museum of Man*, June 1991
Moriarty, James R., *Professor Anthropology and History, University of
San Diego*, November 1990
Sampson, Michael, *State Archeologist Southern Region, California
Department of Parks and Recreation*, January 1991
True, Delbert L., *Professor Anthropology, University of California,
Davis*, July 1991

PRE-GOLD RUSH AND MEXICAN PERIOD
Emory, William H., *REPORT ON THE UNITED STATES AND
MEXICAN BOUNDARY SURVEY*, Cornelius Wendell, printer, 1857
Lake, Stuart N., *BIRCH'S OVERLAND MAIL IN SAN DIEGO
COUNTY.*, San Diego Historical Society Quarterly, April 1957
Bancroft, Hubert Howe, *HISTORY OF CALIFORNIA*, 7 Vols., The
History Company Publishing Co., San Francisco, 1886
Hayes, Judge Benjamin, *EXCEPTIONS TO THE SURVEY OF THE
CUYAMACA GRANT, BEFORE THE SURVEYOR-GENERAL OF
CALIFORNIA.San Francisco*, A.L. Bancroft & Company, 1873
Pitt, Leonard, *CALIFORNIA CONTROVERSIES*, Scott, Foresman
and Co., Glenview, Illinois, 1969
Robinson, W.W., *LAND IN CALIFORNIA*, University of California
Press, Berkeley 1948

CIVIL WAR & Julian and Bailey Service Records
Bryan, T. Conn, *CONFEDERATE GEORGIA*, University of Georgia
Press, Athens, Georgia, 1953
Crute, Joseph H., *UNITS OF THE CONFEDERATE STATES ARMY*,
Derwent Books, Midlothian, Virginia, 1987

Dowda, Julius L., C.S.A. DIARY, Co. "F" 3rd Ga. Cav., Army of East Tenn., 1868, Georgia State Department of History & Archives, Atlanta, Georgia

Foot, Shelby, interview, THE CIVIL WAR, AN ILLUSTRATED HISTORY, Alfred A. Knopf, Inc., New York, 1990

Henderson, Lillian, ROSTER OF CONFEDERATE SOLDIERS FROM GEORGIA, Georgia State Department of History & Archives, Atlanta, Georgia

Jasper, James, HM&TB

McPherson, James M., ORDEAL BY FIRE, Alfred A. Knopf, New York, 1982

McPherson, James M., BATTLE CRY OF FREEDOM, Oxford University Press, New York, 1988

NORTH CAROLINA TROOPS, 1861-1865, A ROSTER, Compiled by the North Carolina Department of Archives and History, Published by the University of North Carolina Press, 1943

Wiley, Bell Irvin, THE LIFE OF JOHNNY REB, Louisiana State University Press, 1943

MICHAEL S. JULIAN, Biographical References:

Bagley, Garland C., HISTORY OF FORSYTH COUNTY, GEORGIA, Two volumes, Southern Historical Press, Inc., Easley, South Carolina, 1985

Jasper, James, A. HM&TB

Long Beach (Calif.) Independent Press Telegram, September 21, 1958

HISTORY OF LONG BEACH AND VICINITY, The S.J. Clarke Publishing Company, Chicago, 1927

LONG BEACH CITY DIRECTORY, 1899, 1900 and 1902

JULIAN AREA - GENERAL

Ellsberg, Helen, MINES OF JULIAN, La Siesta Press, Glendale, California, 1972 (revised 1986) (MOJ)

Grand, Fred, NOTES AND REMEMBRANCES ABOUT JULIAN, addressed to author, April, 1990

Jasper, James, TBAHM & JARA

Julian Historical Society, HISTORY OF JULIAN, 1969

Mallow, Wally, JULIAN'S COUNTY SEAT ELECTION OF 1873: Legend or Reality, Typescript, 1973, San Diego Historical Society Collection

Sawday, Ruth Cornell, JULIAN -- GOLD TO DAFFODILS, typescript, author's collection.

Sheldon, Gale W., JGMD
Taylor, Dan Forrest, JULIAN GOLD, Federal Writers Project, 1939,
   unpublished manuscript, Julian High School

MINING
Bollon, Herbert Eugene, SPANISH EXPLORATION IN THE
   SOUTHWEST, 1542-1706, New York, Charles Scribners Sons, 1916
California State, Division of Mines, Bulletins issued 1888-1926 and
   Reports issued 1881-1927, California State Printing Office,
   Sacramento and San Francisco.
Ellsberg, Helen, MOJ
San Diego County, Dept. of Agriculture, Division of Natural Resources,
   Ninth Annual Report. San Diego, 1952
San Diego Daily Sun, 1/22/1898
Sheldon, Gale W., JGMD

CUYAMACA GRANT & BOUNDARY DISPUTE
Crane, Clare B., THE PUEBLO LANDS: SAN DIEGO'S
   HISPANIC HERITAGE, Journal of San Diego History, Spring 1991
DESCANSO, PLACE OF REST, Published by the Friends of the
   Descanso Library, 1988
Hayes, Judge Benjamin, EXCEPTIONS
Robinson, W.W., LAWYERS OF LOS ANGELES, Los Angeles Bar
   Association, Los Angeles, 1959
San Diego Union, running coverage from May 1870 through January
   1874
United States Land Commission and US District Court
   Proceedings, Cuyamaca Rancho Grant case files, University of
   California, Bancroft Library, Berkeley
Willardson, Mary, THE FLUID BOUNDARIES OF THE
   CUYAMACA RANCHO, typescript, 1979, San Diego Historical
   Society Archives

CUYAMACA RANCHO STATE PARK
Bloomquist, Richard A., A HISTORY OF CUYAMACA
   RANCHO STATE PARK, Calif. Dept. of Parks and
   Recreation, Sacramento,   1966-1968
Rhodes, Warren, THE HOUSE OF STONE , Cuyamaca Rancho
   State Park Interpretive Association, 1983

Rodgers, Frank Kent, *CHARLES LELAND WEBBER*, Journal American Aviation Historical Society, Winter 1990
Mason, Herbert Molloy jr., *THE UNITED STATES AIR FORCE, A TURBULENT HISTORY*, Mason/Charter, New York, 1976
Interview with Granville Martin, by California Dept of Parks and Recreation, edited by Daniel Foster, June 2, 1981
San Diego Union newspaper

STONEWALL MINE & CUYAMACA CITY
Ellsberg, Helen, MOJ
McAleer, H. John, *STONEWALL MINE AND CUYAMACA CITY*, State of California, Dept. of Parks and Recreation, Sacramento, 1986
Sheldon, Gale W., JGMD

SCHOOLS
Julian Apple Day Booklet, October, 1965, published by the Julian Chamber of Commerce
San Diego County, *SUPERINTENDENT OF SCHOOL RECORDS*, San Diego Historical Society Archives

WATER
Fletcher, Col. Ed., *MEMOIRS*
The Ed Fletcher Collection, University of California, San Diego, Calif. Letters from T.S. Van Dyke, J.D. Howells, M.A. Luce and Joseph H. Smith addressed to Fletcher 1919.
LeMenager, Charles R., *OFF THE MAIN ROAD*, Eagle Peak Publishing Company, Ramona, California 1983
McConoughy, O.H., *THE SAN DIEGO FLUME*, The Golden Era, San Diego, Calif., December 1888
Pourade, Richard F., *THE GLORY YEARS*, Union Tribune Publishing Company, San Diego, 1964
Scientific American, March 15, 1890
Wilson, Herbert M., *IRRIGATION ENGINEERING*, John Wiley & Sons, Inc, New York, 1914

AGRICULTURE
Hutchinson, Juli & Joe, *JULIAN APPLE STANDS*, Julianjo Co., Julian California, 1987
Jasper, James, JARA
Jasper, James, TBAHM

Acknowledgements

We wish to thank the following organizations and individuals for their help, leads, material, pictures, information and in general, their most kind assistance. Books like this represent a lot of detail work and material gathering and without the help of many people, they just aren't possible.

ORGANIZATIONS
CALIFORNIA DEPARTMENT OF PARKS AND RECREATION,
  San Diego Office
GEORGIA STATE DEPARTMENT OF HISTORY AND ARCHIVES
  Atlanta, Georgia
JULIAN CHAMBER OF COMMERCE
JULIAN HISTORICAL SOCIETY
LONG BEACH (CALIF.) HISTORICAL SOCIETY
RAMONA PIONEER HISTORICAL SOCIETY
SAN DIEGO COUNTY DEPT. OF PARKS AND RECREATION
SAN DIEGO GENEALOGICAL SOCIETY
SAN DIEGO HISTORICAL SOCIETY
SAN DIEGO MUSEUM OF MAN
CALIFORNIA ROOM, SAN DIEGO PUBLIC LIBRARY
SOUTHWEST MUSEUM, Los Angeles
BANCROFT LIBRARY, UNIVERSITY OF CALIFORNIA, Berkeley
SPECIAL COLLECTIONS LIBRARY, UNIVERSITY OF
  CALIFORNIA, San Diego

INDIVIDUALS
Tom Adamo, Woody Barnes, Jacque and Darrell Beck, Leland Bibb, Jane and Larry Booth, Patrick Brown, Mable Carlson, Michael Judson-Carr, Rick Crawford, Hugh Crumpler, Bud Farmer, Willis Fletcher, Dave Goodman, Fred Grand, Ken Hedges, Alexandra Luberski, Wallace Macfarlane, James Moriarty, Chuck Oldsen, Susan Painter, Milo and Lelah Porter, Charlotte Ray, Ray Redding, Frank Rodgers, Billie Rassmussen, Rick Robertson, Michael Sampson, Charles and Ruth Sawday, Jack Shu, Raymond Starr, Delbert True, Mary Ward, Sally West, Guy Woodward and last, but not least, for his special help, Richard Zerbe.

PHOTO CREDITS

BANCROFT LIBRARY, UNIVERSITY OF CALIFORNIA,
BERKELEY, p.69; W. BARNES COLLECTION, p. 141;
HUGH CRUMPLER COLLECTION, p. 209; ED FLETCHER
COLLECTION, p. 153; FRED GRAND COLLECTION,
pgs. 136,183,& 184; H. NELSON COLLECTION, p. 143;
LONG BEACH HISTORICAL SOCIETY, p. 58;
RAMONA PIONEER HISTORICAL SOCIETY, pgs. 105,125;
FRANK RODGERS COLLECTION, p.197;
SAN DIEGO HISTORICAL SOCIETY,
pgs.47,53,54,69,93,95,101,104,108,111,121,122,131,135,146,147,149,156
158t&b,159,161,167,169,182,185b,189,190,192,193,211b & 217b.
SOUTHWEST MUSEUM COLLECTION, p. 29
BALANCE OF PHOTOS BY THE AUTHOR

ILLUSTRATION CREDITS

ROSE CHRISTENSEN, pgs.18 & 19; JULIAN CHAMBER OF
COMMERCE, p.14; DELBERT TRUE, p.25; UNIVERSITY OF
CALIFORNIA, EXTENSION, p.41; FREDERICH T. CHAPMAN,
p.46; COUNTY OF SAN DIEGO, DEPARTMENT OF
PLANNING AND LAND USE, p.138; ERNEST PRINZHORN,
COVER

Index

ABOUT THE AUTHOR

Charles LeMenager is by profession a businessman and land use consultant. In recent years, however, he's spent more time at his avocations - researching and writing history, photography and piloting his Cessna Cardinal airplane.

He came to San Diego County in 1970 to help master plan and develop the new community of San Diego Country Estates in San Vicente Valley near Ramona. He and wife Nancy liked San Vicente so well they've made it their home ever since.

Local and state government have also occupied much of his time for over thirty years, although mostly as a sideline. He is a former mayor and councilman in the City of Santa Rosa, California, a California State Director of Housing and Community Development and member of the Ramona Municipal Water District board.

The view from his office not only takes in the beautiful San Vicente Valley, but the three Cuyamaca Peaks and Eagle Peak as well and helped inspire this book.